A SIMPLE SOUL

MOVING FROM FEAR TO LOVE

by Kimberly Cowherd

This is a memoir. This book is the sole copyright of the author and can't be reproduced in any form without the sole permission of the author. To contact the author for these permissions or other engagements email the publisher:

editors@emerald-books.com

BISAC Categories:

BIO000000	BIOGRAPHY & AUTOBIOGRAPHY / General
BIO026000	BIOGRAPHY & AUTOBIOGRAPHY / Personal Memoirs
BIO016000	BIOGRAPHY & AUTOBIOGRAPHY / Sports
BIO022000	BIOGRAPHY & AUTOBIOGRAPHY / Women

Summary:

This is the story of my journey and some of the lessons I learned. My lessons have come through the experiences of playing competitive sports, years of running and competing in triathlons, going through a couple of marriages, having children, discovering the beautiful practice of yoga, and juggling life itself.

Copyright © 2021 Kimberly Cowherd

All rights reserved.

ISBN: 978-1-954779-11-2
Cover art made
with photos by Zhang Kaiyv
and Madhavan R. licensed
through Unsplash.

TABLE OF CONTENTS

DEDICATION	IV
INTRODUCTION	V
CHAPTER ONE:	
CHILDHOOD AND BASKETBALL	1
LESSONS BASKETBALL TAUGHT ME	8
CHAPTER TWO:	
RUNNING AND HUSBAND ONE	40
LESSONS RUNNING TAUGHT ME	49
LESSONS LEARNED GOING THROUGH A DIVORCE (THE FIRST TIME)	71
CHAPTER THREE:	
TRIATHLON AND HUSBAND NUMBER TWO	78
LESSONS FROM THE IRONMAN EXPERIENCE	89
LESSONS LEARNED IN TRIATHLON	97
CHAPTER FOUR: YOGA	116
CHAPTER FIVE: MANIFESTING	138
CHAPTER SIX: SPRING CLEANING	147
CHAPTER SEVEN: QUOTES AND BOOKS	154
SOME OF MY FAVORITE BOOKS	160
INSPIRATION AND GIVING BACK	161
ACKNOWLEDGMENTS	165

DEDICATION

*M*oving through life, many events have inspired me to be a better version of myself. They have molded me and touched my heart in ways that keep me growing spiritually. One constant factor in my life that has brought me endless joy is the unconditional love of my parents, Joe and Florence Vadala. My father passed in September 2019, but I know he is looking down on me smiling and full of pride.

I dedicate this book to my parents who created me and exposed me to experiences molded me into who I am today. I am eternally grateful for their love, kindness, acceptance, and support. They dedicated much of their lives not only to raising three children, but to helping others. They passed the torch to me; now it's my mission to touch as many lives as possible. Thank you for everything, Mom and Dad. I love you both with all of my heart and soul.

INTRODUCTION

Let me take you on a journey. Grab a cup of coffee or tea, get comfortable in your favorite reading space, and let's begin. We ALL have a story. Some are filled with more pain and suffering than others, but we all are broken somehow. We live in a world of extremes. We are an all-or-nothing society; we are judged for our successes and our failures. I don't look at failure as many others do. I consider failure an experience that didn't work out exactly how we planned. What we learn from these experiences helps us grow and gives us new perspectives on life. The reality is that we all have expectations, and when our expectations aren't fulfilled, we may feel disappointed. If we don't try and sometimes more than once to meet those expectations, we fail. When we fear failure, we stay in our comfort zones and avoid risks. The downside to that approach is that we don't grow; we

deny ourselves the chance to flourish. What would you do if you knew you could not fail?

Often, we function in a world of "I'm right, and you're wrong." Egos get in the way when they serve as defensive mechanisms. Things seem either black or white, and many people are not comfortable in the grey area. However, my life experience has brought me to where I am, where I'm meant to be. My successes and failures prepared me for the next steps in my life. I share my story, successes, failures, and joy and pain to inspire you and demonstrate that we are all connected. We all want love and acceptance. Unfortunately, life is challenging and complex. Such experiences can harden our hearts and souls and keep us from the love we deserve. Life can be simple, yet we find a way to make it more complicated.

When I graduated from college, I had two things on my bucket list. One was to run a marathon, and the second was to write a book. I ran my marathon the year after I graduated from college, and now, almost 30 years later, I'm finally writing my book.

At first, I wasn't sure what I would write about. The first thought I had was simple; we all have a story. The idea came to me when I was a spin instructor in Connecticut. Teaching spin was like my two worlds colliding. I was a DJ in college at our college radio station. I had my show, *The Soul Show*, every Sunday night from ten to midnight. I played R & B for two hours and was in heaven. I love to exercise, so what could be better than being a DJ on the bike? It was the perfect job for me!

    I taught at a gym that had a fantastic spin room. We had 55 bikes. I taught three classes a week, and my class was almost always full. One day, I looked up and thought, *Everyone in here has a story*. We all have our pain and suffering, joy, and happiness. No one is better than any other. Although we all come from different walks of life and are different in many ways, we have much in common when it comes down to it. We all want to be loved and accepted. Group classes connect people. We feed off each other's energy. It's my job to give each student a fantastic experience, to connect with them, and to facilitate their connections with one another. I was humbled that each person took the time to come to my class. They were all there for different reasons. They came to burn calories, relieve stress, take their minds off something else, or get

A SIMPLE SOUL

away from the kids for an hour. Whatever their reason, it was my job to give them what they came for. I enjoyed motivating my students with stories about my personal experiences. I love things that inspire me; I love people with energy because they are inspiring. I wanted that dynamic in my spin classes, and I believe I created it. It was so much more than the physical part of the workout. I took it deeper, on an emotional level.

Sometimes I felt a spiritual connection, both internally and with some of those in my class. Students came up to me after class, asking if I was a motivational speaker. That always made me smile. They'd tell me I inspired them to start a new business, run a marathon, or do something else that took courage. I shared my experiences so they knew that I was an ordinary woman trying crazy physical things. I wasn't any better or any worse than they were. I wanted to connect with them. I wanted them to see me as one of them.

I feel many instructors sometimes lose sight of the nature of their job. It's not to show their class what good shape they are in, get a good workout themselves, or kill the class. Teaching a good class is about empowering people. The true gift of teaching classes is creating an atmosphere where people feel comfortable, accepted, and wanted, which motivates them to push themselves to work hard and get what they want out of class. The purpose is to motivate them and connect in a way where they want to push themselves to be better versions of themselves. They should walk out of a class feeling better than when they walked in. I wanted them to feel strong, courageous, and confident. If they can get through a challenging hour of spin class, they can get through the rest of their day. They'll carry a sense of strength with them when they leave the class and into the day or days ahead. In the end, when all is said and done, we are all the same. We all have self-doubt and fear the unknowns in life.

    In this book, I share my story and experiences, good and bad, to inspire and connect with others through interactions healing to souls. The book is not intended to be autobiographical, per se. Instead, I share key moments from my life and lessons learned along the way. Various decades of my life shape the chapters in the book. Each chapter shares teachable moments that prepared me for

# A SIMPLE SOUL

the next chapter of life. Each chapter includes happiness, sadness, joy, and conflict. In the end, the experiences led me to where I am today and gave me the strength and courage to know I can face anything in the chapters of my life that are unwritten. I ultimately want to share experiences to share the lessons I've learned from those experiences.

I am now 50 years old and entering a new chapter in my life. As a single mom with two children (twenty and fifteen), I can say I am happier than I've ever been. I am at peace with myself, and I have created a life of balance and flow. It was quite a journey to get where I am, and I know I still have a long way to go. My feeling of success comes from within. It's not related to how much money I have, the house I live in, or the car I drive. It's nothing material at all. My feeling of success in life stems from internal things. I have built a life for myself that is peaceful and calm. However, it wasn't always that way.

At one point, I needed to simplify my life physically, emotionally, and spiritually. I needed to move from any fear-based energy I had to a love-based, emotional state of mind. I did this after the divorce from husband number two. I left a 5,000 sq ft home, country club lifestyle, driving a Cadillac, and downsized to a 1,700 sq ft townhouse. I took my clothes, my children, and a few belongings and started over. I wanted to free myself from some of the material things in my life. It was just stuff.

It was liberating to leave almost everything behind and begin a new chapter in my journey in life. This chapter is one of peace, clarity, and simplicity. The road to get here has been rough at times, but I know deep down it all happened to get me to this point. All the joys have filled my heart with love, and all the sadness has given strength to take on the next challenge.

Before I share how my journey began, consider two emotions: fear and love. Both are real, affecting our decisions, thoughts, and feelings, and we can control them. More specifically, we can control how we respond to our emotions.

Fear-Based feelings include self-doubt, insecurity, change, unknown, vulnerability, failure, loss of control, racism, negativity, pain, scarcity, panic, dismay, distress, anxiety, worry, trepidation, dread, unease. Love-Based feelings include acceptance, trust, forgiveness, compas-

sion, empathy, openness, vulnerability, kindness, letting go, surrendering, embracing, liberating, appreciation, gratitude, mindfulness, intention, tenderness, warmth, gentleness.

We all have reached the point where we are in our lives right now because of decisions we made, stemming from both logic and emotion. Logically, we can talk ourselves in or out of anything. We can justify our choices and our decisions based on logical facts at that time. I've learned to grow emotionally. Emotions can paralyze us and also invigorate us, depending on where these emotions are coming from. Are they coming from fear or love? Just like our energy, we are positive or negative. Are we moving toward positivity or negativity? Are we moving toward love or away from it? When we move away from love, we move toward fear. When we move toward love, we move away from fear. It's that simple. Hopefully, this book will make you think about the direction in which you've been moving, along with other life lessons.

KIMBERLY COWHERD

"Have faith in your journey. Everything had to happen exactly as it did to get you where you're going next!"

—Mandy Hale

CHILDHOOD AND BASKETBALL

BCHS was my high school (Boulder City High School) shooting guard. Kim Vadala is my maiden name. Spartans was the team of the community college I went to, Western Wyoming Spartans.

CHAPTER ONE

CHILDHOOD AND BASKETBALL

"Life is a journey that must be traveled no matter how bad the roads and accommodations."

—Oliver Goldsmith

My life began on June 18, 1970, in a small town in New Jersey. I grew up in Rockaway in a strict, Italian-Catholic family. If you haven't spent time with Italians, you haven't experienced what loud is. Everyone in my family was loud. My father was a strong, vocal, Italian man and my mother is everything but Italian. As a kid, I never felt that I fit in with our family. I was the youngest of three children and the only one who played sports. I loved to be doing something like climbing trees, building obstacle

 A SIMPLE SOUL

courses in the backyard, or whatever. I wasn't much of a girly girl.

My Italian family loved to gather and eat. I remember family gatherings with endless amounts of food. Back then, nutrition wasn't something people talked about. We ate lots of pasta, bread, and of course Italian desserts. My parents struggled with their weight their whole lives. My dad's weight fluctuated up and down many times, and my mom was on different diets. One particular experience shaped how I thought about weight and affected my relationship with food.

I was in the sixth grade and attended a Catholic school. On the first Friday of the month, the school organized a "hot dog day." Order slips were sent home with all students the week before. The kids filled out the forms and brought money in for their pre-ordered hot dogs. The volunteer moms made and served this lunch in the church basement cafeteria. My mom always volunteered and loved being involved with the church and school activities. She worked two jobs at times but somehow found time to volunteer. During lunch on one of our hot dog days, a girl came up to me and said, "You have a fat mom.

KIMBERLY COWHERD

My mom is skinny; why is your mom fat?" I was speechless. I didn't respond. Instead, I turned and walked away. That broke my heart. My mom was the kindest, most generous person I knew, so for someone to say something so hateful was devastating. I told myself that day that I did not want to be a fat mom. Moving forward, I remember periods during which I didn't eat for days. I was extremely mindful of what I ate, how much I ate, and what I looked like. The girl's comment changed my relationship with food forever.

Food became my enemy. I feared being fat. To this day, I'm aware of my relationship with food. I think many girls and women struggle on some level with food and/or body image. Unfortunately, how we look and feel about ourselves affects our self-esteem. Our society doesn't help with this either! We are continually exposed to thin-people images everywhere we look, such as magazines, television, movies, social media, etc. I have finally developed a healthy relationship with food, and it is not my enemy. From an early age, though, we are programmed to look a certain way, and with my family's history of weight problems, I was afraid of being fat. Not

 A SIMPLE SOUL

for health reasons per se but because of appearance. As an adolescent, I learned that by being active, I could control my weight with exercise.

When I was in the seventh grade, I discovered basketball. I didn't love it at first, but after I started playing, I realized it came pretty naturally to me. I was the high scorer for my team. By the eighth grade, I had set the goal of playing basketball in college. During my freshman year of high school, my family moved to Boulder City, Nevada, a small town outside Las Vegas. It was a culture shock. I had a thick Jersey accent, and no one else did. I wondered why Nevada people talked funny. I realized I, too, had an accent. I lost it quickly! It was a difficult move, but as long as I had sports, I was good. Basketball became my outlet. When I was playing, I felt like I could be myself. As I mentioned, I wasn't a girly girl. Basketball allowed me to be aggressive and scrappy. I could run, sweat, and compete.

Back then, we didn't have travel teams to join, which gave players access to coaches year-round. At least, I didn't. Instead, I'd take a ball to the closest park and shoot and dribble by myself for hours. One high school coach told me that guards were a dime a dozen, and I would never play in college. He said I was too short and too slow. I knew I wasn't very tall. I'm 5'6" but slow? Really? That moment was pivotal. Those words motivated me to do what I said I wanted to do. I love it when people think I can't do something. I love the nay-sayers and doubters. I love the challenge of trying to prove them wrong!

Starting in my junior year, I practiced all summer long and in the offseason. I ate, drank, and slept basketball. I had one coach (he wasn't the one who said I was too short and too slow) who would open the gym for me on summer mornings a few days a week for a few hours. In Nevada, summer temperatures could get up to 115 degrees. Brutal! So, having access to an indoor gym was amazing! After dedicating endless hours to shooting and dribbling, my hard work paid off, and I was recruited to play college basketball at three small colleges. I chose a community college in Wyoming because they offered a full scholarship. I'd rather be a big fish in a small pond anyway.

I was team captain both years and named player of the year for my division one year. After two years, I was

A SIMPLE SOUL

recruited to Southern Utah University in Cedar City, Utah. It was a small, Division 1 school, but again, a free ride is a free ride. I majored in Communications with an emphasis in Radio and Television Broadcasting. I finished the next two years there, playing basketball. To this day, I still hold the free-throw record with 88.2%. I was never a great player, but I worked hard and stayed positive no matter what. For most of the years that I played basketball, I was team captain, but I never thought of myself as a leader. I wasn't a follower, but I never saw myself as having strong leadership qualities. I did my thing, and people seemed to follow my lead.

I loved the attention I received for my successes in basketball. My family gave me support and attention. Both parents were incredibly loving and giving people. My mother could give Mother Theresa a run for her money. Since they did so much for other people, at times, I did feel loved by them. Looking back, I realize my feelings were far from the truth, and there was enough love to go around. As a young girl, I thought they wanted to give their attention and love to strangers and not to me.

KIMBERLY COWHERD

When I played basketball, I never felt so good! I received attention and praise. It filled any void of not feeling loved and gave me the attention I needed at that time. Playing ball gave me a sense of purpose and developed leadership qualities in me. The lessons I learned playing sports prepared me for the challenges I would face in my life. Some of the lessons and values that I learned playing 10 years of basketball are as follows.

 A SIMPLE SOUL

LESSONS BASKETBALL TAUGHT ME

1. *DEVELOP A STRONG WORK ETHIC*

HARD WORK PAYS OFF. What you put into something is what you get out of it. The basketball season is pretty long. It starts in October or November and continues through March. That's a lot of months of hard work. That doesn't include the pre-season, which is mainly conditioning. It starts in August and runs into the start of the actual season. Practicing day in and day out takes dedication and discipline to yourself, your teammates, and coaches. Some days you are more motivated than others. Showing up for practice every day and working your best, whether you feel like it or not, requires a work ethic. Many sports develop a work ethic in athletes, and basketball is no exception. I'm a big believer in what you put into something is what you get out of it. Going through the motions will get you nowhere. There will always be someone more talented or naturally gifted. Still, if you are willing to work harder than they do and have the discipline to do that, you will be successful. It's not easy to practice hard every day, doing the same drills (some of which we hated) with 100% effort and enthusiasm, but if you can discipline yourself, you will succeed in life. I often think it's as simple as that.

As a society, I don't feel we are very disciplined. We can be lazy and expect things to be handed to us. Many people are not willing to work hard and sacrifice to live a disciplined life. They feel entitled to something. This sense of entitlement can be the demise of anyone's success. Life can be simplified. What do you want, and what are you willing to do to get it? Are you willing to sacrifice or even suffer? Are you willing to put in countless hours of dedication and hard work? Are you willing to get up and keep going even when you fall? Are you willing to push through adversity?

It sounds like an easy concept, but so many people struggle with discipline. Many people aren't willing to work hard and sacrifice to get what they want. The more time and energy you put into something, the better you will become. The 10,000-hour rule applies here. In, *Outliers: The Story of Success*, Malcolm Gladwell claims that if you do something for 10,000 hours, you will achieve true

expertise in that skill. If you want to be a better shooter, you need to shoot for hours. If you're going to be a better ball handler, you need to practice ball handling for hours. To be good at anything, you have to commit time and energy to that task. Ask yourself, "how disciplined am I in life? In what areas can I be more disciplined?"

2. WORK AS A TEAM, TRUST YOUR TEAMMATES, AND KNOW YOUR ROLE

WITH ONLY FIVE PLAYERS on the court at a time, trusting one another is essential. Trusting your teammates to be in the right place at the right time isn't easy. Basketball is a game that involves mistakes. We call them turnovers but limiting the number of them is the goal. You and your teammates will make mistakes but trusting that they meant to do the right thing involves confidence on your part. When they make a mistake, you must trust that it wasn't on purpose, and you can forgive and move on. When a teammate forgets to cut after a pass, trust means you assume they did not forget on purpose. Yelling at teammates doesn't do any good. It destroys trust among team members. When I see players yelling at each other on the court, it suggests they don't trust each other. If they did, the exchange of words would be more positive. "Hey, you forgot to cut after that last pass. Let's get it right the next time."

We all make mistakes. I'm sure that the player didn't cut to be a jerk. Trust that they know what they are doing

A SIMPLE SOUL

and that they will get it right the next time. Trusting people is empowering, and it takes practice and a conscious effort on each person's part. It entails giving up control. On the basketball court, one person cannot do it all. Players rely on teammates to perform in other areas such as rebounding, bringing the ball up, and making good passes. Each player must know her role if the team is to be successful. That's why trust among teammates helps everyone perform to the best of their ability. Every role on the court and the bench is essential. The team is as strong as its weakest player.

Trusting requires giving up some power and control, which few people want to give up. Learning to trust allows us to experience so much more in life. Think of the times when we trusted someone, and they came through, and we experienced love and joy. When they did something untrustworthy, we felt hurt and pain. Instead of building the wall to avoid that pain, we need to understand that pain is part of life. We have to feel the pain to appreciate joy! Ask yourself," How trusting am I in others? Do I trust myself? The universe? How can I practice or improve in trusting others and/or myself?"

3. WHEN YOU KNOCK SOMEONE DOWN, OFFER TO PICK THEM UP

Show good sportsmanship all the time. Offer to pick players up even if you're not the one who knocked them down. This takes the emotion out of the game. Basketball is one of the most emotional, intense sports I've played. If we can take some of that emotion out, then whatever happens on the court becomes about the game itself rather than the people playing it. Some players struggle to see the sport that way, and therefore emotions can take them off their game. We cannot control many things on the court and in our lives. However, we can control our emotions. If we spend our time and energy worrying about what we can't control (the refs, the other players, people in the stands, etc.), we lose sight of our focus. Channeling energy into what we can control is productive. We can control our emotions and attitude. How we respond to things and how we react is what matters. Taking the high road in a situation is the best thing to do. When you knock someone down, walking away demonstrates a bad attitude even if you're not in the wrong. Pick them up! We

A SIMPLE SOUL

need to pick more people up, both the ones we knock down and the ones we don't. Ask yourself, "Am I quick to pick others up if I knock them down? Do I pick others up even when I don't knock them down?"

4. PLAY BOTH OFFENSE AND DEFENSE

TO BE GOOD AT SOMETHING, you have to dedicate time and work hard to what you're trying to be good at—practice, practice, practice. Balance matters, too, however. You can't merely practice shooting. You have to play both ends of the court. Every player wants to score, but that's only part of the game. It's all the little things that contribute to a win: assists, rebounds, defense, etc. If a player is one-dimensional, they are easy to shut down. Learn to be a threat no matter where you are on the court. The same applies to life generally. If we just focus on one aspect of our lives, we become one-dimensional. Life requires achieving balance, but it's not easy. Balancing school, family, friends, and a sport is challenging. Still, if you learn to do that early in life, you can apply the skill as an adult when things get more complicated, and stress is higher.

One of the best books I've read is *Oola - Finding Balance in an Unbalanced World* by Dave Braun and Troy Amdahl. I came across this book a few years ago. It was in my goodie bag from a triathlon I did in Las Vegas. I've never had a book in my goodie bag before. They are usu-

ally filled with samples of power bars, sports drinks, and coupons. This book was the best thing I could have read at that time. The book suggests balancing all aspects of life as though they are saucers on a stick. If one plate starts to slow down, it'll fall and break, so we have to give it a spin to keep it going. The plates represent seven areas in our lives, the 7 F's: family, friends, finance, fitness, faith, fun, and field. When you think about it, how often do we let one or two areas in our life slip? It's tough to keep everything balanced and in alignment, but if we don't, that is when we feel the stresses of life build up. It's a lifelong challenge but necessary for peace and harmony within us.

Balancing ourselves as individuals is as essential as balancing life emotionally, physically, professionally, mentally, and spiritually. Sports (and basketball) teach us to work on every aspect of our lives. If not, we become weak in an area, and therefore that area suffers. We have to play both ends of the court. It's not just about scoring. The defense wins games. However, you don't always get recognition for playing good defense. A coach told me, "you don't get your name in the paper for playing defense." In other words, the leading scorer gets most of the recognition. Therefore, I took his advice and didn't hesitate to shoot. As a shooting guard, playing defense was my primary job. Still, I also knew that when my outside shot was off, I had to drive more to create a higher percentage shot or play more formidable defense to get some steals so I could score off the lay-up. Knowing I had to play both ends of the court required that I strategize about scoring; I needed a plan.

Life, in part, requires a plan. Having clear ideas about what you want to accomplish in life is imperative to success. Many people say, "I knew when I was a kid what I wanted to be," and they are usually doing just that. When we go through the motions in life with no direction, we end up lost and unaccomplished.

In basketball, you can't just run up and down the court. You have to try to be involved in every play. You can't just go through the motions. If you are not involved in every play, ask yourself why you are not. Realistically, being involved in every play might be a stretch. Still, there is merit in knowing how many times you run up and down

the court without being involved. Such awareness may change how aggressively you approach the next play.

Similarly, in life, consider whether you are merely going through the motions. Do you make 100% effort each day? If not, why not? Are you playing both sides of the court? Are you living a balanced life? Where can you improve?

5. PLAY TO WIN BUT LEARN HOW TO LOSE GRACEFULLY

PLAYING TO WIN SOUNDS OBVIOUS, but it's more complicated than it sounds. When you play to win, you put 100% on the table for the whole game. All the hours, weeks, months, and years of preparation come down to game time. When the ref blows the whistle and tosses the ball, the game begins, and your primary goal is to win. We don't train hard day in and day out to lose. It is essential to go into a game intending to win even if you are outmatched. Sports teach us that anything can happen, to any team, at any time, so everyone is beatable. Although I played the game because it's fun, winning was always the goal.

That said, "winning at all costs" is not what I'm advocating. Good sportsmanship always takes precedence. But it helps to have the mindset that when things get tough, you have to stay focused and dig deep. When you get tired toward the end of the game, you have to keep winning in mind. The team that wants it more generally wins. They will do what it takes to win. Typically, athletes

A SIMPLE SOUL

with this mentality are gracious losers as long as they played with 100% effort and didn't leave anything on the court. A loss is inevitable at times. Learning to lose graciously can be challenging. It's hard to put your heart and soul into something and end up defeated. If we take that defeat and channel it into the next game, we will come out fighting in the next one. Losing invites us to reflect on what we did wrong or the mistakes (turnovers) we made. But that's only half of it. Changing and improving on what went wrong is how we grow. The same holds true in life. When we are struggling or defeated, we need to reflect and adjust accordingly. It's not always easy to identify and admit our weaknesses, but if we do what it takes to improve those weaknesses, we will grow. Sometimes our pride or ego get in the way. Ask yourself, "Do I play to win every time? Do I graciously accept defeat?"

6. MAKE YOUR FREE THROWS

MY BIGGEST PET PEEVE is missing free throws. There is no excuse. They are FREE. No one is guarding you. You have time to set up and shoot. Free throws come down to two things: routine (repetition) and focus.

You need to have the same routine each time you shoot. Whether it's three dribbles, a spin, then shoot or two dribbles, deep breath, and shoot, whatever the routine is, do it every single time. Picture the ball going in every single time—repetition, repetition, repetition. Focus is something we can control. Learning to keep your head in the game takes energy and practice. Often, athletes let the pressure get the best of them. Relaxing and shooting with confidence help when it comes to shooting free throws. Breathing deeply and slowly relax the mind and body, so taking a few breaths helps. Just like meditation helps with centering and clearing the mind, a few deep breaths help with free throws.

Many games come down to free throws at the end, so it's crucial to make them. In life, jump on opportunities when they arise. Don't let "free" opportunities pass us by.

A SIMPLE SOUL

No one wants regret. Opportunities are free passes to try something new and to grow. When asked what they regret the most in life, many people regret what they didn't do, not what they did. I have few regrets because I view my questionable decisions as learning experiences. I have learned and grown from them. I have tried to create a world of opportunity, not letting much pass me by. I usually do what I want to do instead of worrying about why or whether I should do it. I prefer a "Why not?" approach. Do you take advantage of all the opportunities that life brings you? Do you let things pass you by or say no to opportunities because of fear?

7. SET GOALS—LONG AND SHORT TERM

MANY PEOPLE STRUGGLE to set goals. They may set unrealistic goals, or they don't have a plan to achieve the goal. When we set goals, we have to look into the future and imagine where we want to be. Goals force us to "dream." I believe we should set goals higher than what we think we can do. Often, we underestimate our abilities and set goals that are comfortable. Generally, we live in our comfort zones. When we step out of our comfort zones, we experience things we probably never would have dreamed imaginable. When we try something new, we set ourselves up to change and grow.

Often, we fear change, we fear negative experiences, and we fear the unknown. Fear stifles us! By setting goals, we move in a direction that may be unknown or frightening. Both long and short goals keep us focused and give us direction. We must look to set short-term and long-term goals. In basketball, you may have an immediate goal individually or as a team. For example, the coach may want to work on defense, so when scrimmaging, we focus on getting at least five steals. Individually, let's focus on shooting at least 40% from the field. On the court, immediate goals give us direction "today." Off the court, having a goal or trying to accomplish something is important. Goals keep us focused day to day and allow us to move with purpose and intention. Not allowing things to pile up in our lives but breaking down daily tasks is imperative to goal setting. The steps you take to achieve the goal are as necessary as the goal itself. Setting goals and planning their execution keep us from feeling overwhelmed or helpless. It forces us to prioritize our goals and work on the most important thing.

How often do we wake up in the morning asking, "What do I want to accomplish today?" That's step one. Step two is taking the appropriate action and following through. I like to let my friends and family know my goals. When others know, they keep you accountable. Just like a coach keeps the team on track to obtain their goals, having supportive people checking in on you can help. Ask yourself, "What are my goals? What are my short-term goals? What are my long-term goals?"

8. BE AGGRESSIVE

IN SPORTS, YOU HAVE TO PLAY AGGRESSIVELY. You have to jump on your opponent right from the beginning. If your shot gets blocked, you do not stop shooting. You learn to keep going at it. Off the court, we have to be aggressive in how we are actively moving toward our goals. We must do what we need to do, day in and day out, to get what we are striving for. We can't take "no" for an answer. Many people fear rejection, so the word "no" can be devastating.

In the ninth grade, my son had to watch a TED talk about the fear of rejection. The story was about a young man from China who wanted to be an entrepreneur. He had an opportunity to move to America to pursue his dreams. He realized that his fear of rejection was holding him back. So, he dedicated 100 days and looked for opportunities to be rejected to get used to it, hoping it would desensitize him from the pain of rejection. He picked a person each day and asked that person a question, to which he thought the answer would be "no." He asked a homeless man for $100; he asked a cashier at a fast-food

A SIMPLE SOUL

place for a burger refill. He asked a Krispy Kreme donut shop to make an Olympic ring out of donuts—they replied YES. It was so inspiring for my son. He said he wanted to try the fear of rejection challenge. That only lasted two days with two rejections, but the story's moral was taken to heart. His follow-through is what we'll need to work on next!

The saying, "It's not how many times you get knocked down that count; it's how many times you get up, that counts." We will inevitably get knocked down, rejected, or fail. We all do at some point in our life. The question is, how quickly do we get up? We all get up eventually. What matters is how long it takes us to get up.

A college coach made us run suicides at the end of practice. We would shoot a free throw, one player at a time, and she would count our misses. The number of misses was how many suicides we had to run. If you've never run a suicide, you're missing out in life. We would line up on the end line, she would blow the whistle, we would sprint to the free-throw line, touch it, turn around and sprint back to the end line, bend down, touch it, turn around and sprint to the half-court line, touch, and sprint back, to the other free throw line, touch, and sprint back and then to the other end line, touch, and sprint back. We had to do this in under 35 seconds which we usually did.

One practice, the coach decided to mix it up. Every time we touched the line, instead of turning and sprinting back, we had to backpedal back, essentially running backward. I'm sure you can imagine where I'm going with this story. On the last suicide, I tripped and fell. I put my right hand back to break my fall, and all my weight landed on my wrist. I lay there for a moment in excruciating pain. I knew I had done something to my wrist. While the team continued to run, I began to sit up only to hear my coach yelling, "Get up! What are you going to do if you fall in a game? Just sit there?" So, of course, I got up and continued to run while I held my wrist. She told me to finish the suicide. I was the last one to cross the line. She looked at the time and said, "Kim didn't make it in time. Looks like we have to do another one. If we don't make this one in 35 seconds, we'll keep doing it until we do." I thought, "How ruthless can this woman be?" I sucked it up, though. Holding back the tears and trying not to think

about the pain, we all did the next one under 35 seconds, so we were done.

The next day, I woke up to a wrist and hand that looked like a balloon. They were bruised and swollen, so my coach took me to the doctor. My wrist was broken. I think my coach felt a little bad for making me run with a broken wrist. Once the cast went on, she made me continue to practice using my left hand, which was a blessing in disguise. My left-hand lay-ups got much better. When it came time to run drills, she would say, "Your legs aren't broken; you can run!" Which was true. As uncompassionate as I thought she could be at times, she was right about many things. We can't sit and cry for too long. The quicker we can pick ourselves up, the sooner we can move on.

Basketball taught me to be aggressive and to keep playing as long as the ball is in play. Don't back down no matter what and pick yourself up quickly to move to the next play. If you miss a shot, you don't hang your head and walk back on defense. You shake it off and go for a steal, or somehow make it up defensively. Ask yourself, "Am I aggressive with my goals in life? What am I trying to achieve? How long do I stay down before I pick myself up after I fall?"

9. WHEN YOU MAKE A MISTAKE, MOVE ON

I TOUCHED ON THIS PREVIOUSLY, but I want to emphasize the importance of this lesson. This is a lesson that we can use in every part of our life. What are you hanging on to? What holds you down? What holds you back? You may or may not know the answers to these questions. That's ok. Start thinking about them and bring more mindfulness to your life in the process. Usually, fear or not wanting to make a mistake prevent us from moving forward, especially after making a mistake. We know the feeling of making a mistake, again, but mistakes are inevitable. Once we accept that we are not perfect, nor are we supposed to be perfect, we can move on with a little more empathy and kindness for ourselves. I say it all the time; we are our own worst enemy. We are so hard on ourselves. Why? Is it the pressure of society? Is it to prove something to ourselves or others? We need to understand that we are not built to be perfect and never make mistakes. I'll say that once again. We are not built to be perfect and never make a mistake. In basketball, "mistakes" are called turnovers. The goal isn't to have zero turnovers. That's unrealistic. The goal is to keep the number as low as possible. But once we make a turnover, we can move on and not dwell on the error.

So, too, in life, we must not dwell on negative experiences or emotions. We must not carry such feelings into other parts of our day or other aspects of our lives. They become baggage that grows heavier the longer we carry it around. We have to learn to let go and move on.

I am amused when people claim that something or someone ruined their day. How can one person or one thing take away the joy that the rest of the day might have brought? I will never let either anyone or anything ruin my day. It may ruin a moment or several minutes of my day but giving up my power for a whole day is bizarre. Don't let people or situations take away your happiness. We control our thoughts and, to some extent, our emotions. We can control our reactions to these emotions. People can create a feeling for you, but you choose how long you want to keep it, or you can choose to let it go. Ask yourself, "Can I let go of things easily? Do I hang on to anger or resentment? How quickly do I move on?"

10. RESPECT THE OFFICIALS AND THE COACHES

This lesson brings value to our lives. We use the word respect all of the time. The term is often used, but do we know what it means to respect someone or something? Respect is "a feeling of deep admiration for someone or something elicited by their abilities, qualities, or achievements." Politeness, courtesy, and civility are synonymous with respect.

When I talk about respecting coaches and officials, it's fair to say that we are talking about treating these authority figures with courtesy, politeness, and civility. We might not have admired specific authority figures in our lives in ways that accord with the definition of respect. Still, we treated them with courtesy, politeness, and civility.

Growing up, I was taught to respect my elders. In today's world, we embrace the notion of questioning and not taking things at face value. In some respects, this is good. We don't just follow. We question to understand. In some ways, we lost the importance of respecting others and treating people with kindness. We often do not value

A SIMPLE SOUL

everyone's opinions and perspectives on life. We tend to lose sight of humanity.

As a player, we were taught that we should not question a call or talk back to a ref when the official makes it. Accept it and move on. It is the coach's job to question or challenge a call. The player's job was to play. We were taught that the officials would make some bad calls. We would also get some calls in our favor. That's the way life goes as well.

As a player, I never had issues with officials or coaches. I respected that they knew what they were doing, for the most part, and they were doing the best they could. As a coach, I was amazed by how many of my players didn't always grasp this concept. I usually had a talk at the beginning of the season with the team, going over housekeeping rules/expectations. I always emphasized as a coach that I would make decisions throughout the season about when we would practice, how long we would practice, what drills we would do, who would play, and who would not. Players liked some of my decisions and some they didn't. Remember, it's not that they necessarily had to agree with my decisions. I asked only that they respect them and thereby support me and the team. We were all in it together, so we needed to support each other regardless of whether or not we agreed. I made decisions in the best interest of the team. If they disagreed, it was fine. Players could talk to me, and I would explain my perspective. I was okay with that, but I did not want to hear complaining. Negative energy brings everyone down. It's a privilege to be on a team; it is not a right!

As my coaching progressed through the years, I was hired as the head coach of a varsity high school women's basketball team in West Hartford, CT. The school was Kingwood-Oxford, a highly prestigious preparatory school. The annual tuition was $35,000. Needless to say, I saw many entitled mindsets from both the girls and the parents. It was a rough year. I have a hard time with entitlement. Knowing how hard I worked athletically to get where I got, I couldn't grasp that because you pay an extraordinary amount in tuition, you are entitled to whatever you want, especially playing time. In my eyes, there is so much that goes into who gets to play: how hard someone works in practice, who brings positive energy to the team, who can get things done, etc. I was the head coach for

A SIMPLE SOUL

one year there, and I was not a good fit for that culture. Toward the end of the year, I wrote a letter that I wanted to send to a local newspaper, which I never did. I'll share it here.

> *I write this letter as a coach of 20 years, a competitive athlete of 30+ years, a mom, and a spectator. I have many points of view, but the bottom line stays the same. Here is my perception of where sports today are going.*
>
> *As parents, we all want the best for our children. We don't want to see them hurt or struggle, but as a parent, we need to let them struggle and hurt at times. Both will make them stronger people. Isn't our goal as parents to create productive and strong people who will contribute to society?*
>
> *Sports teach so many life lessons for our children, but I think we need to be reminded from time to time what those lessons are. One is to work hard, every day! Work hard in practice and games. Two is to support your teammates. Don't be envious or jealous of who is getting playing time. Is that being supportive? No, it's negative, and it*

brings everyone down. It brings terrible energy to the team. If you're not happy with the amount of playing time, do something about it. Work harder in practice, play on weekends, in the offseason, or whatever it takes to earn playing time. If you're not playing, there's a reason. Talk to your coach. Don't have your parents say a word to your coach or athletic director about playing time. Unless your child is being abused (physically, emotionally, or sexually), let the coach do their job, and that's to coach. Keep your mouth shut! Nothing but positive comments should come out of parents' mouths.

The coach has dedicated time, energy, and wisdom to this team. Unless you think you can do a better job, get your coaching certification, and coach the unit yourself. I feel we have lost all respect for coaches and teachers, for that matter. These people are professionals. Let them do their jobs.

Give them the respect they deserve. Trust me, every parent has an opinion. The coach can't listen to every parent's opinion. If you think you have all the answers, coach the team yourself. What message are we sending to our kids if every time they don't like something, we step in as parents and complain? We are producing nothing but negative, complaining, entitled kids who are never happy. If they are not happy on a team, try a different sport.

I would love to see the day where kids play sports to be competitive, to be pushed, and challenged, to play to win, and to learn to be a team player, when you have to earn playing time, that life Isn't always fair, to push through adversity, and to be dedicated to themselves and teammates.

Unfortunately, I see sports today as something parents want their kids to do to keep them busy. Many parents live through their children. Not all kids should play sports, just like all kids shouldn't take AP Physics. I see parents upset that their little Johnny or little Jane doesn't get to play as much as the other kids. Not everyone should play, but that doesn't mean they are not enjoying their experience as a valuable part of the team. Maybe your son/daughter enjoys taking the role of a supportive teammate, and playing time isn't their concern.

Now is an excellent time to reflect and be thankful for what we have. Be grateful that we have coaches who have dedicated time to our children. Be grateful that our kids are on a team. If we constantly look at what's wrong in this world, we will never appreciate what's right. Let's just watch our kids experience sports, however that is for them, and tell them these three things every day: I love you, have fun, and play hard.

Ask yourself, "How do I show respect for others? Even if I disagree with someone's opinion, do I treat them with courtesy, politeness, and civility?"

"If you are willing, great things are possible to you."

—*Grenville Kleiser*

RUNNING AND HUSBAND ONE

Colin Cowherd and I in our dating years

My first marathon on October 1, 1994. St. George Marathon in St. George, Utah.

CHAPTER TWO

RUNNING AND HUSBAND ONE

"I hated every minute of training, but I said, don't quit. Suffer now and live the rest of your life as a champion."

—Muhammed Ali

I discovered a different level of running after I graduated from college. Having played sports all of my life, I knew that I had to keep my fitness level as a priority in my life. I also met my first husband, Colin Cowherd, at this time. He hired me as an intern at the NBC affiliate TV station. He was a sportscaster, and my degree was in Radio and Television Broadcasting. I thought I wanted to be a sports reporter. When I graduated, I sent audition tapes to all the major affiliates in the Las Vegas market, ABC, NBS, and CBS. Colin was the only one who responded and called me in for an interview. After a few months of working the internship, I realized it wasn't the profession for me, so I went back to school to get my master's in education to teach and coach (girls' basketball, of course).

I was waitressing full time and attended UNLV. This was when I started long-distance running. I loved every part of it. After a few months, I knew I needed a goal to train for, so I picked a marathon. Not a 5K, 10K, or even half-marathon. No, let's do a marathon! Go big or go home, right? Since I was living in Las Vegas, Nevada, at the time, I wanted to pick a marathon that wasn't too far away. I registered for the St. George, Utah marathon that would take place on October 1, 1994. It was January, so I had nine months to train. In hindsight, nine months was way too long to train. I learned from that mistake. I would also not pick a marathon in the fall again because that means the peak training months are in the summer.

Las Vegas in the summer can get to 115 degrees. I had to do my long runs at 4 am to be done by 7 am, when it might be 90 degrees already. Lesson learned! I subscribed to *Runners World* and submerged myself in the running mindset. I bought Jeff Galloway's *Book on Running* and began my training. I must say training for a

marathon was similar to playing a sport. All those years had prepared me for marathon training. I had a goal. I showed up every day and did what was intended for that workout. I had the discipline to do what was expected of me that day regardless of how I felt physically or emotionally. It gave me a structure. I loved it! My goals were simple: I didn't want to walk under any circumstances, and I wanted to finish in under four hours.

The best advice I received was from a triathlete friend of Colin. He had done several Ironman races. If you're not familiar with Ironman, it's a 2.4-mile swim, followed by 112 miles on the bike, and then a marathon, 26.2 miles. Crazy, huh? Why would anyone want to do that? I'll tell you in the next chapter.

He told me to start slowly. He said to run the first three miles super slow. When you think you're running slow, slow down. I listened. My perception of this man was that he was a workout machine, and I better take his advice. After racing for years, I now give that same advice when I coach. It's easy at the beginning to feel great and take off at a quick pace. It takes discipline to start slow and get behind from the beginning. But his philosophy was that a marathon is a long way to run, 26.2 miles long. He said that most of those people who bust out the first few miles will end up either walking or slowing down halfway through. He said to let them go and run your race, super slow the first three miles, then gradually pick up the pace until mile 6, then find your rhythm. He was exactly right. People took off like they were running the 50-yard-dash. I did exactly what he told me to do. Back then, I didn't wear a watch, so I went off the clocks along the course to figure my pace. If I wanted to run this race under 4 hours, I had to run just under 9 min/mile pace. The race started on a negative note, though. Again, back then, when the gun went off at the start, the clock started, and so did your time. They didn't have chip timing.

Now, you wear a chip around your ankle which tracks your time as you physically cross each timing pad on the course, giving an actual, accurate time. Back in 1994, the gun went off, and your time started even if you were at the back of the runners. Unfortunately, I was in the port-a-potty when I heard the gun go off. I scrambled to pull my shorts up, get some hand sanitizer, and run out to the

A SIMPLE SOUL

back of the pack. Boy was my adrenaline going, but I remembered the advice to start slow! So, I slowed down.

When I got to the first clock on the course, which was at mile three, my time was just under 30 minutes. Yikes! I had run slowly. Part of me panicked, thinking I have to make up the time since I'm averaging just under a 10-minute mile. But his words stuck in my mind. Gradually pick up the pace for the next three miles, then find my rhythm. I ran the next three miles a little faster but not too much. I found my rhythm at mile six. Around the half-marathon mark, thirteen miles, I ran near a guy about my pace, so we started talking. I don't remember his name, but this guy was my best friend for the next 7 miles.

We talked about where he was from, what he did for a living, and how many marathons he had completed. I kept asking open-ended questions to keep him talking and distract me. This turned out to be a strategy I used in future races. Pick someone close to my pace, start up a conversation, and ask open-ended questions until they either got faster or slowed down because I was annoying them. It passes a lot of time and keeps me distracted from the pain. It worked many times! Since Utah was his 4th marathon, I figured I'd just stick with him, and he'd help me finish. At mile twenty, however, he told me he was going to walk. I almost cried. I told him he couldn't walk, and he had to stay with me to the end. He kept reassuring me that I'd be fine and to keep going. Not what I wanted to hear.

The following six miles sucked! I was all alone, and things started hurting. I felt muscles I never knew I had. I kept positive thoughts in my mind, but this was probably the most mentally challenging thing I'd done up to that point in my life. I kept telling myself, just get to the next mile marker. Breaking it up one mile at a time helped. This got me through the next few miles. I reminded myself of my goals: don't walk and finish under four hours. I added up all the miles I had run to train for that marathon, and it was over 1,000! Again, I trained way too long, but it was my first, and I learned that I didn't need to train that long for the next ones. Rookie mistake. But I said to myself at that point, "I didn't run over 1,000 miles to quit now!" That gave me the motivation to push through the pain. I used that strategy in many of my upcoming races too.

A SIMPLE SOUL

I remember seeing the twenty-five-mile marker, and the clock read 3:33. Holy shit, I'm going to do this in under four hours! Again, not wearing a watch, I didn't know what my pace was. I knew I felt like shit and couldn't wait to get to the finish line. The advice given to me was perfect. Once I saw that 3:33 time, I started picking up the pace. I don't know how I mustered up the strength to run faster, but I did. It must have been adrenaline that took me in since I couldn't even feel my legs at that point. I crossed the finish line with a time of 3:40. That's 3 hours and 40 minutes. I had done it! I ran the last mile at a 7 minute-mile pace passing many, many people. It was the most exhilarating feeling. Colin and my parents were at the finish line, and seeing them brought tears to my eyes. What an emotional experience. I was thrilled with my accomplishment. After training so diligently for 9 months, crossing that finish line was one of the proudest moments I've had.

Something about running clicked with my soul. I could be with my thoughts, feel my breath, feel my body, and just go away from everything. Looking back, maybe I was running from something but at the time, running saved me. It was my release, my way not to think about anything or the opposite, think about everything, and work problems out in my head. I could get lost in my thoughts. I continued running through my twenties, thirties, and forties. I was fortunate to compete in six marathons, dozens of half-marathons, along with endless 10Ks and 5Ks.

But along with all that running, I had several injuries. You name it, I had it: plantar fasciitis, pulled Achilles' tendon, hip flexor strain, etc. As much as I loved running and what it did for me mentally and physically, I knew something needed to change. Too much of anything, even if it's good, isn't good. I should have stopped at one marathon, but I wanted to see if I could better my time given my competitive nature. Running became my addiction. I believe that we all need outlets, and some of us fall into addictions to help soothe the pain of life or the past. Exercise became mine. Having an addictive personality, I'm glad I chose exercise as opposed to alcohol, drugs, food, sex, gambling, etc.

Something else about running was also very appealing to me. I liked the feeling of breaking myself down to build back up. It felt cleansing. Long runs were so therapeutic that way. It's the feeling of cleansing the mind, body, and

A SIMPLE SOUL

soul on these invigorating runs. Finding a balance for me to have an outlet or release but not addiction has always been an underlying theme given I partake in. I tend to be an all-or-nothing type of person. When I'm in, I give 110%. Learning balance is always a work in progress in my life. Running was no different. But I learned so much from all those years of running.

LESSONS RUNNING TAUGHT ME

1. SET GOALS

WORK TOWARD YOUR GOALS with a plan in place. Train with a purpose. In our life, we need a purpose and a plan. I try every day to wake up with my list of "to do's," prioritize this list and have a plan for how I'm going to accomplish the tasks at hand. When we live with this intention, it's easier to stay focused and keep life's big picture in sight. Ask yourself, "What am I doing to reach my goals? Do I have a plan? Am I on track, and what corrections will I take to make sure I reach my goals?"

2. LISTEN TO YOUR BODY

AS A RUNNER, you must take days off. Most runners do not want to take too much time off because they worry that they will lose fitness. But the body needs rest to grow stronger. We need days to do nothing without guilt. It's not lazy to rest. If we don't get proper rest, we put ourselves at risk of overtraining, potentially leading to injuries.

Once I came close to rupturing my Achilles tendon. I ran for years on an injured foot that was only getting worse. Finally, I went to a doctor who told me to stop running for three months. I did not want to take his advice. However, I knew if I didn't, I could tear my Achilles tendon. The doctor warned me that if the tendon tore, it would require surgery to reattach it. That would mean I'd be on crutches for months with no running at all for at least six months. Even after it healed, running at the level I was at might be questionable. So, I grudgingly listened to his advice and didn't run for three months. I used the elliptical trainer, took spin classes, swam, and practiced yoga, so I got my workouts in. I pledged to focus on what I could do rather than on what I could not do. That focus helped me get through three months without running. The injury healed enough that I returned to running. However, the tendon still hurt from time to time. The years of running through the pain had caused serious and irreversible damage to the tendon. Taking time for rest would have been the smartest thing I could have done.

Before I took three months off, I ran the relay race called Hood to Coast in Oregon. It was held every August, and I had run it every year that we had lived in the area. It was a two-hundred-mile, twelve-person relay that started at Mt. Hood and ended in Seaside, Oregon, on the coast. Each team had two vans with six people in each. Here's how it works. Van One heads out first. The first runner runs their leg, usually between four to eight miles, and then hands off a baton to the second runner until all six runners have completed their legs of the race. Once Van One occupants complete their legs, the sixth runner hands off the baton to the first runner in Van Two, and the process repeats itself. Van One drives to the following van exchange, where the runners have time to stop, eat, and sleep before Van Two finishes its six legs of the relay.

 A SIMPLE SOUL

The two-van exchange occurs continuously through the night and into the next day. The occupants of each van cheer on other runners along the way. It is wonderful to have runners in vans other than one's own cheering as they drive past. Some teams dress in costume, and every team decorates their van. The race is like a big party that revolves around running. I was on a competitive team of all women. Our team usually finished under twenty-four hours, which was pretty fast, and we usually placed in all women's divisions. Most of the women on my team were serious runners, many of them sub-seven-minute milers. Some ran competitively in high school and college. I am not sure why I was on that team since I was one of the slowest runners, averaging around 7:30 minute miles. I like to think I made up for my lack of speed with my energy and positive attitude. I brought the music and the dancing, so our van was recognized as the fun, sporty van!

The year that the race preceded my three-month hiatus from running, I ran two of my three relay legs pretty hard, and by my third leg, I could barely walk. My heel was a shade of red I've never seen before. It looked angry. My heel was so swollen from all the years of microtears that scar tissue had built up to a lump the size of a golf ball. My teammates named the lump of scar tissue "Henry." "Henry" was furious that day, and the relay was the last race I ran for a while. I had not listened to my body, and it almost cost me a torn Achilles tendon.

The moral of the story is that if your body needs a rest day, take it. Better yet, take a rest day before your body begins to ask for one. One missed workout isn't going to make or break a runner. The benefits of training are cumulative. Rest is part of the training. By the same token, it is crucial in our non-running lives to listen to our bodies and honor what they need. Such attentiveness is vital to our physical, emotional, and spiritual well-being. We need breaks and downtime to re-energize. Still, how often do we let ourselves get run down, overwhelmed, and anxious? These feelings indicate that it is time to pay attention to our environment and the stresses that life imposes on us. The bottom line is that we must take care of ourselves. No one else is going to do it for us. Practicing good self-care is not selfish; it is wise.

 A SIMPLE SOUL

To that end, I ask the athletes I coach how much sleep they get. Although it should not surprise me, usually they are not getting adequate sleep. Everyone requires a different number of hours of sleep to function optimally. Still, many of us share in common chronic sleep deprivation. If we need an alarm to wake up, chances are our bodies are not getting enough sleep. We should wake up naturally at more or less the same time daily. I require a minimum of eight hours of sleep. I'm shocked when I hear of people who function on only five or six hours of sleep. Sleeping gives our bodies time to repair themselves. Even if one is not training for a race, one's body needs to reset and recuperate from life's daily stresses. We must monitor the extent to which we pay attention to our bodies' physical, mental, and spiritual needs.

3. DEVELOP SELF-DISCIPLINE

THIS IS ONE OF THE BEST LESSONS I learned early in life. I consider myself highly disciplined. I'm not the most talented athlete, but I had the discipline to work hard every day regardless of what was going on in my life. Hard work and diligence pay off. I'm an example of that. I wasn't highly talented or gifted athletically, but I worked my tail off and had a positive attitude. Effort and attitude are always within our control. We carry discipline into many aspects of our lives, such as our finances, our diets, and our time. I'm grateful to have learned that early. Discipline is when good habits become habitual. It takes fourteen days of doing something daily to make it a habit. So, if we dedicate two weeks to a particular practice, we will find it easier to be disciplined in that sector of our lives. Consider the areas in your life where you might be more disciplined.

 A SIMPLE SOUL

4. Don't try to avoid discomfort; accept it and work through it

At mile twenty of a marathon, everything hurts. That is when to tell yourself to grin and bear the pain, to keep going, and to embrace all that you're feeling—anything that keeps you moving forward. Many addictions in our lives stem from trying to avoid discomfort rather than feel our way through it. Working out allowed me to escape some of life's pain, even though the relief was temporary. I preferred to bear physical pain than mask my inner pain. As I said earlier, we all are broken somehow; we all have pain from the past. But we need to heal. As the saying goes, "time heals all wounds." Many of us don't have the patience to let time heal us. We want the pain to stop, so we mask it with our addictions. Running taught me to work through physical discomfort, but we must also learn to work through our emotional pain as well. We need to feel emotions, even the negative ones, and let ourselves pass through those negative emotions to grow and move forward in our lives. Masking pain with things like drugs or alcohol is merely a temporary solution. Consider the areas of your life where you may be masking your pain instead of allowing yourself to feel it. From what are you trying to escape? If you conceal what you're escaping, how long will you have to keep escaping it? Are the masking agents you choose sustainable agents in the long run? Are you strong enough to take a healthier approach by feeling the pain and working through it?

 A SIMPLE SOUL

5. *Pain is temporary, pride lasts forever*

ALLOWING OURSELVES TO FEEL PAIN ties in with being disciplined. If you do things for the right reason, setting the ego aside, things will work out. Inevitably, we'll have challenges and challenging times in our lives. It is important to remember that they will pass. Everything in life is temporary. The only sure things are taxes and death.

Live each day with intention and a strong work ethic, and the resultant pride will carry you through the pain and joys of life. As with running, when the pain becomes unbearable, remember that stopping or quitting will stay with you forever. Feeling the pain will bring you pride that you'll carry forever. Ask yourself, "How easily do I give in to the pains of life? Do I practice positive self-talk, telling myself that whatever I'm going through is temporary?"

6. BREAK DOWN YOUR RUN, ONE MILE AT A TIME

LEARNING TO BREAK CHALLENGES into components has helped me tremendously in everything I do. When I teach spin classes, I break up the hour with songs. I remind people that we're working on one song at a time. I remind them that they can do anything for three or four minutes. It holds true with fitness, your professional life, and tasks that need to get done. Procrastination is a terrible thing, and I think most people procrastinate because they feel overwhelmed. So, they put tasks off because they do not know where to start. Some tasks can feel daunting but breaking them into manageable components and tackling them one at a time makes a task more manageable. Getting started is half the battle. Ask yourself if you get overwhelmed easily. Do you take time to break overwhelming projects into smaller components?

 A SIMPLE SOUL

7. BALANCE WORK, FAMILY, FRIENDS, AND FITNESS

BALANCE IS A CRITICAL COMPONENT of life. I learned that you have to keep everything balanced when you're a mom, who has a job, a husband, and friends. They are all crucial aspects of life, and the challenge is to keep all these aspects balanced. Feeling overwhelmed is usually a sign that we are overextended in one area. It's easy to neglect certain parts of our lives. We have to manage every aspect of our lives, or it won't be long before we feel overwhelmed or unbalanced. We need to assess what we are neglecting or where we are directing too much attention. Analyze the degree to which your life is balanced. Ask yourself if you're giving each area of your life proper attention? Don't wait until things spiral out of control before assessing what is out of alignment.

During my years as a runner, I married Colin. I was twenty-five years old. He was offered a job in Tampa, Florida, where he worked as the weekend sports anchor and weekday reporter at the Fox affiliate TV station. I was hired as a middle school teacher teaching seventh and eighth grade in a program called ILAP (Intensive Learning Alternative Program). I taught English, Math, and Geography to about eighteen students who were pulled from the mainstream class because of behavioral problems. I was their last hope before expulsion. I had a counselor in the classroom with me at all times, but it was a challenging first job as I had just graduated from college.

Since Colin worked weekends, I took a job as a weekend manager at a running shoe store. The other employees were primarily runners, too, mostly running for their high school or college. I always ran solo; that was my time. However, the store organized group runs on Wednesday evenings. I was a more "get in a rhythm and run miles and miles" runner.

In contrast, the store's group took off and kept an aggressive pace for miles and miles. The lead runners casually ran their six-minute mile pace, talking and laughing along the way. I was always at the back of the pact, huffing, and puffing, just trying to keep up. When I first joined the group, my goal was to keep the other runners in sight and not fall too far behind. After a few weeks, it got easier to keep up, and my times improved. I was still at the back of the pack, unable to add to the conversation, but I kept up, nonetheless. The moral of the story is that to get faster, it helps to run with people who are faster than you are. By the same token, to improve in any area of life, it is helpful to surround ourselves with people who have more expertise in the area we want to improve. Surround yourself with people who will push and encourage you to perform increasingly better.

I started my refereeing career officiating high school basketball, which I loved. I never had any problems with the kids; I had issues with the parents, who tended to do little more than shout out negative comments. No matter what call I made, someone complained. As an official, I expect the coach to ride me; that goes with the territory. But the parents' hostility was unbelievable. I officiated for several years, but in the end, I loved coaching more. The upside to officiating was that I developed a thicker skin than I had previously. I made my calls, and that was that. Regardless of parents' or coaches' negative comments, I knew I made the best calls I could and moved on.

Developing a thicker skin also helped me in my coaching career. Officiating gives one a different perspective on the game they are refereeing. As a player, I knew what the game felt like from the court, and as an official, I called the game as I saw it from a non-biased perspective. Coaches don't necessarily see everything and, like the players, are emotionally invested, unlike officials. So, when I moved into more of the game's coaching part, I took what I learned from playing and officiating and used those perspectives to strengthen my coaching skills and benefit my teams.

After two years in Tampa, Colin was offered a job in Portland, Oregon, at the NBC affiliate television station. There, he worked on TV and on the radio. Both Colin and I loved Portland and the Pacific Northwest. One of the best memories of my life is of the day our daughter was born. I was in the hospital just starting labor, so Colin went for a run. It was a perfect, sunny September day in Portland. There were several nice neighborhoods close to the hospital, so Colin ran through them. At one point, he looked over at a yard where two girls were playing in the grass, and it was as if time slowed down for him. Maybe he slowed down to notice the girls, but he described the scene as though it were a picture from a story

in which two girls were giggling and running in the front yard. When he returned to the hospital, he walked by the nurse's station, and one of them asked if we were having a boy or a girl. We did not know because we'd wanted it to be a surprise. It felt as though much of our lives were structured and planned at the time, so the irony of being able to plan a surprise did not escape us. We thought it would be amazing to discover the sex of our child at the moment of birth. Of course, the sex is never that much of a surprise. It's not like a turtle is going to pop out of someone.

At any rate, Colin told the nurse that we didn't know if the baby was a girl or a boy. She asked what names we had in mind. He started with a list of girls' names: Olivia, Lauren, Sydney, and Morgan. One of the nurses paused in reflection and said, "Olivia Grace, what a beautiful name." At that moment, Colin knew we were having a girl and that we would name her Olivia Grace. He knew that because "Grace" was the middle name we'd had in mind, but he hadn't told the nurse that. When the nurse responded to Colin's list of names, Colin sprinted into the room and told me, "It's a girl, and her name will be Olivia

Grace!" That was the name I was pulling for, so there were no complaints on my part.

As labor progressed and my contractions grew more intense, I could tell Colin was extremely uncomfortable seeing me in such pain. Initially, I was going to see how long I could tolerate the pain before having an epidural. When I told my doctor my plan, he looked at me and said, "Kim, you get a medal for running a marathon. You don't get a medal for having a baby. Get the epidural!" His point was not to be a hero by tolerating as much pain as possible before asking for relief. At that point, I was only dilated three or four centimeters. Still, the pain was horrible, so I asked for the epidural. The epidural was a game-changer. I felt pressure but no pain.

.

I knew I could do this. As the hours passed, however, I began to feel incredibly intense contractions. Something was wrong. I called for the nurse. She came with the anesthesiologist in tow; she adjusted the lever controlling the amount of medication I was receiving and told me to wait while it took effect. After fifteen minutes, the only things that kicked in were more painful contractions. I

couldn't believe how severe they were. I went from feeling nothing to feeling excruciatingly painful contractions. My body went into shock; I threw up and sweated profusely. It was horrible! I kept reminding myself that the pain was temporary and that I could get through labor. Also, I recall wondering whether having a baby or running a marathon was harder. The pain was pretty comparable. I told myself, "running the marathon trained me for labor. I can do this!"

Colin had eaten a sandwich earlier that day, which must have been loaded with mustard. He apparently thought continuously blowing on my face to cool me down would be helpful. Mustard breath is never helpful and definitely not during labor. The poor guy was trying to help. Classic Colin! The medical team finally realized that the epidural was disconnected. The anesthesiologist reinserted it and the pain subsided shortly after that. Olivia Grace was born in the early hours of September 12, 2000. It was definitely one of the best days of my life!

Colin continued to work extremely hard, trying to further his career. His efforts at work, however, took a toll on our marriage. I felt as if we had different life goals.

None of our goals were right or wrong; they were merely different. It tore me up to think of breaking up our family, but I wasn't happy with the direction in which we were moving as a couple. Deep down, I knew I was a simple soul. I had always felt that as long as I had a workout and a coffee, my day was bound to be good! Colin's career was something he had desired since childhood, and he worked extremely hard to achieve it. He wanted to be the best at what he did, and he was willing to sacrifice whatever it took to get it.

While living in Portland, I decided to give up my teaching career. I took my Series 7 test, similar to the bar exam in law and insurance license, to become a financial planner. I followed that career path for five years. I loved helping people reach their financial goals. I also coached girls' basketball at a middle school in Portland. Trying to balance work, both jobs, being a mom, being a wife, a social life, and fitting in my workouts became more challenging as time went on. I became overwhelmed and felt entirely alone at times. Colin was doing very well in his career, but he worked two jobs, which meant we didn't see each other much. The lack of time together took its

toll. When our daughter was two, we divorced after much inner turmoil.

I had been raised Catholic, and divorce wasn't an option. I kept telling myself to stay married for the sake of our daughter, and that life wasn't that bad. It was true that looking in from the outside, life wasn't that bad. My husband made good money, we lived in a beautiful neighborhood, and we took nice vacations. Still, I wasn't happy. Now, I assess situations when I'm at a crossroads using the 75/25 rule. I list the pros and cons and the positives and negatives. If I have at least 75% positives, then I figure it is like buying a house. We can't get everything we want, but if we can get at least 75% of what we want, that's quite good. Of course, looking at a relationship isn't that simple. Relationships aren't about the pros and cons. Ours was about how I was feeling inside and the degree to which I felt I was growing. It did not seem that we were growing in the same direction. We went to counseling for months, looking for guidance to help us grow as a couple. It seemed to help temporarily. I read some self-help books, trying to figure out why I wasn't happy. I beat myself up for a long time over not being satisfied. Was the marriage that bad? Was I being selfish?

The shame and guilt I carried with me about wanting to leave what others saw as a good marriage were gut-wrenching. I was afraid of what our friends would think, what our families would think, and most importantly, being the initiator, knowing I would hurt Colin terribly. I felt like a failure. I felt as though I had failed myself, Colin, and my new family. As a competitive athlete, failure wasn't an option. I also felt very selfish about my decision, but I knew deep down that it was the best one. Colin needed a wife who was in the marriage for the right reasons. I felt that staying for our daughter's sake wasn't enough. I cared for him deeply, and I guess that's why, when we decided to split up, I still treated him with respect and kindness, as he treated me. Still, next to running a marathon and giving birth, going through a divorce was one of the most painful things I've done.

Grief and mourning go hand-in-hand with the process of a divorce. The relationship, one that you put your heart and soul into, was dying. I was despondent. It was hard to understand my sadness because I was initiating the split.

A SIMPLE SOUL

Despite initiating the divorce, however, I was still losing my husband, my friend, and the father of my child. There was a lot of loss. I felt extremely confused and cried endless tears throughout the process.

We divorced, but after about six months of living separately, we tried again and got back together. We bought a new house and tried to start over. Within a few months, Colin was offered a job at ESPN in Connecticut. It was a job offer he couldn't refuse. The pay was better, and Colin would only work on the radio. That meant he would have only one job! I had given up my financial planning practice, and I was only coaching at the time, so it was an easy move for Olivia and me. We packed and moved.

We were still technically divorced, so we remarried. This time it was a short ceremony. I'm embarrassed to say this, but we remarried in Las Vegas at a drive-thru. We had been visiting my family and met some friends for the weekend. A few drinks into the evening, our friend Trace suggested we get married. We found the closest drive-thru and tied the knot again. I was tempted to order a chocolate shake and fries. I didn't think the man officiating the ceremony would find that request funny. Then, off to Connecticut, we went!

KIMBERLY COWHERD

LESSONS LEARNED GOING THROUGH A DIVORCE (THE FIRST TIME)

1. *STAY STRONG*

AS HARD AS IT IS telling someone who you love and who loves you that you don't want to be married to them anymore, stay strong, and trust your decision. I had many moments of self-doubt where I wondered if I was doing the right thing. I questioned whether I was being selfish, as I mentioned earlier. I questioned whether things between us were terrible enough to warrant divorce. These days I say, "do things for the right reason, and in the long run, things will work out." Ask yourself if following through will allow you to stay true to your integrity. Are you following your heart? When things get rough, and I start to second guess myself, do I stay strong?"

A SIMPLE SOUL

2. LISTEN TO YOUR INTUITION

IT'S EASY TO BE INFLUENCED by what others say, what others think, and how people will look at us. In the end, none of those things matter. My mother once gave me the following advice. She said when you go to bed at night, you're the one who has to live with the decisions you've made and will make. If you're not happy waking up to the person next to you, then maybe you need to re-evaluate the relationship. If there are more tears than smiles, you need to make a change.

My mother's advice applies to our spouses and other relationships and also to our careers or jobs. How often do we stay in a situation because it's all we know and comfortable? The situation might not be a good fit for us, but it is familiar, so we stay. The fear of the unknown can be paralyzing. Some people would rather be unhappy but comfortable in a familiar situation instead of making a change that might lead to something better. We don't know what life will be like if we make a change. It is often easier, albeit not necessarily wiser, to avoid making a change because at least the life we know is familiar.

I have learned not only to listen to my intuition but also to trust it. That means trusting myself. I adopted the mindset that any decision I make can be corrected to some extent. So, go ahead and make decisions. Trust that you're making the right ones. If it turns out that your decisions were not good ones, correct them. Assess your decision-making process. Do you trust yourself to make the right decisions? Do you follow your intuition? If not, what stops you from trusting yourself? Do you overthink things? What is the worst thing that could happen if you took another approach?

 A SIMPLE SOUL

3. TREAT YOUR EX WITH RESPECT REGARDLESS OF HOW OR WHY YOU ARE DIVORCING

WHEN COLIN AND I DIVORCED, we vowed to put our child above our egos. We agreed that every decision we made would be in the best interest of our daughter. We have been co-parenting for almost fifteen years now. Our relationship is better now than when we were married. We treat each other with respect. We forgave each other for the mistakes we made, and I made my fair share. But if we could not forgive each other, we wouldn't have been able to move forward in a healthy relationship. Holding on to the past hardens the heart and doesn't allow love to enter. I always had the mindset that I'd only be hurting our child If I were resentful or showed hatred of any kind. Plus, what would I be modeling for her? What kind of an example would I be setting? I didn't want the divorce to be more negative than it had to be for her. It wasn't

her fault that things didn't work out, so why should she suffer the consequences if Colin and I held onto bitterness toward each other. Many people struggle to put

their egos aside and make decisions in the best interest of their kids.

In contrast, instead of holding onto resentment or ill feelings, I wanted to create a happy home for my children and myself. I wanted Colin to make a happy home for himself. To this day, we support each other, and our kids have adjusted as well as they could be expected to adjust. Colin has always been good to me, but most importantly, he's good to our children. If you are going through a divorce or having any kind of antagonistic relationship event, assess how you treat people even when you're hurting or have been hurt. Can you put your ego aside and avoid letting bitterness take over?

"We must accept finite disappointment, but we must never lose infinite hope."

—Martin Luther King, Jr.

TRIATHLON AND HUSBAND NUMBER TWO

Holding my Lululemon photo that was in the local store in West Hartford, Connecticut in 2012.

At the finish line of Fort Lauderdale Marathon on February 2, 2012. Finished but needed some assistance at the finish line.

CHAPTER THREE

TRIATHLON AND HUSBAND NUMBER TWO

*T*his chapter of my life is full of lots of events. Olivia and I moved to Connecticut with Colin so he could pursue his Radio Broadcasting career at ESPN. It was exciting starting over—a new job for Colin, a new state, new friends, and a new life. We talked about having another child. I felt that if it were meant to be, it would happen, and within the year, I was pregnant.

One of the worst moments, however, came less than two months after we found out we were expecting. Colin was with me for an OBGYN visit, and the doctor performed an ultrasound to hear the baby's heartbeat. I will NEVER forget the look on the doctor's face. The room suddenly became hushed, and I knew what she was going to say. She proceeded to tell us that she couldn't find a heartbeat. I knew what she said, but I couldn't comprehend what she was actually telling me. It seemed impossible. Tears ran down my face. Colin was upset, too, but I think it hit me harder. He had to leave the next day for a business trip for a few days. That was horrible. We were far away from our families and hadn't made close connections with new friends yet.

I had one friend who I had met at the gym. I called and asked her if she'd take me to the hospital the following day to have the procedure done to remove the fetus. I had Olivia, who was four at the time, to take care of. She was too young to understand what Mommy was going through. At the time, I was upset that Colin left on his trip, but I knew he had to go to work. He was still trying to establish his career, and I knew what I was getting when I had signed up to be in this relationship. Regardless, it was a challenging experience to go through alone.

Within six months, however, we were pregnant again. In March 2006, our son Jackson was born. Everything was great for a while, but as time passed, the marriage was back to what it had been when we divorced the first time. This time, however, I knew I couldn't keep putting

 A SIMPLE SOUL

band-aids over the problems. We had gone to therapy in the past, but that only temporarily helped us. Moving and having another baby were attempts to stay together, but deep down, I knew we still had different life goals.

Colin's career was everything to him. His passion and drive had been so attractive when I met him and drew me to him. In the end, they were the demise of our relationship. Sadly, we divorced again. The same emotions took over: shame, guilt, sadness, fear. How could I have failed again? I knew I couldn't let my feelings influence my decision. I knew in my heart that I had tried, but the second time around didn't work out as we'd hoped it would. Again, I was heartbroken.

Not long after, I found myself involved in another relationship. It was with Vito, a man who took my spin classes at the gym. We had known each other for years from the gym, but he was married, and I was married, so I never really looked at him that way. I recall a conversation he and I had shortly after my son was born that made me do some serious thinking about my life's direction. We talked after class, and he shared that he had recently celebrated his twentieth anniversary with his wife. At the time, I had been with Colin for about ten years. I thought, "Boy, I hope we make it to twenty!" I asked him what the secret was for a long marriage. He said that he and his wife lived their own lives. They had one son and stayed together for him. Once their son graduated from high school, he intended to leave the marriage. Those words stuck with me. He was merely going through the motions of marriage. I knew I didn't want to be in a position to say the same thing in the years to come. I know many couples who stay together for the children's sake. However, in my heart, I had to stay for the right reasons.

Vito and I connected on many levels. We were both from Italian-Catholic families. We both loved working out, and we both had come out of marriages from which we learned. After only six months, we got engaged and moved in together. I did not doubt that he was perfect for me. Vito was a cyclist, so he got me into cycling. I introduced him to Bikram yoga and triathlon. After all the years of running and many injuries, I knew I needed to cross-train to save my body. Even though I wasn't an outstanding swimmer, and I was new to cycling, I knew my running skills would get me through the race. In my

first few triathlons, I breast stroked the whole distance, which was exhausting! So, after a few races doing that, I put my face in the water and taught myself to swim. It wasn't pretty, but I got it done. The worst part of the swim portion was the claustrophobic feeling. I don't like tight spaces. Putting my face in the water meant not being able to breathe underwater, of course. That, combined with bodies all around me, kicking and flailing, created the conditions of my worst fear! I never got used to the feeling or felt comfortable in the water. I faced fears of those sensations in every triathlon in which I competed.

For the next few years, Vito and I trained together. We competed in races all over the country: Connecticut, Florida, Nevada. We found every excuse to travel and race. We both became quite competitive in our age group. In triathlon, competitors race against others of the same sex in age groups broken down in five-year increments. Competitors' ages are written on their calves in black sharpie before the race, so when they come up behind someone, each person knows if the other is their competition. I was always amazed to see the variety of ages in these races. Triathletes come from all walks of life. As is the case with running, a triathlon is just you with your thoughts and breath for a few hours. I loved the competition part, but I also enjoyed the training and discipline of the sport. Plus, competing in a triathlon forced me to cross-train, so I didn't run my body into the ground.

I later went through USAT triathlon training and became a coach. I loved sharing my passion with others. I trained and coached many athletes for a triathlon. I started with a sprint distance triathlon: a ½ mile swim, 12 mile bike, and a 5Kr run. I graduated to the Olympic distance: a 1mile swim, a 24 mile bike, and a 10K run. Beyond the Olympic distance, the half-ironman is a 1mile swim, a 56 mile bike, and a 13-mile run. Then, it gets fun. An Ironman is an ultimate goal: a 2.4-mile swim, a 112-mile bike, and a 26.2-mile run, which is a full marathon. Now that may sound like kooky talk, but I did it.

The first Ironman I did was in Lake Placid, New York. My best friend, Karen, talked me into that one. We trained together for four months. We spent endless hours swimming at our local indoor pool, on the bike and running. It was great! We talked about our kids, our lives, and everything else under the sun. We'd put the kids on the bus for

A SIMPLE SOUL

school, hop on our bikes, ride 100 miles, and be back in time to meet the kids as they got off the bus. Then it was time for a recovery shake and an ice bath. Good times!

Three weeks before our Ironman race, I went on my last 20 mile run with Karen. I had bought a new pair of running shoes but wanted to get a little closer to race day before running in them. I thought I'd get one more run out of my current pair, which was breaking down. I thought, what's one more run? That was a big mistake! Runners know that running shoes only last about three to four hundred miles. If one is training for an Ironman, that's only three to four months per pair of shoes. Karen and I took off for our three-hour run.

My heel started hurting with 4 miles to go. I didn't want to limp too much because compensating can lead to a residual injury. With 2 miles left, my run turned into a shuffle. I knew something was wrong. We made it back, and I immediately iced my foot. I rested for a few days, but the next run was brutal. I could barely run. I was thinking I had plantar fasciitis, so I iced my foot every day. I took three weeks off running and just swam and cycled. It was time to taper for the Ironman anyway, so I wasn't too upset.

Tapering is cutting back on your distance effort gradually each week, so when race week arrives, you're rested and ready to race. If anything, I swam more, so I felt a little more confident about the swim portion since that's my weakest discipline. There is always a silver lining!

Karen and I went to Lake Placid, bringing our families and making it a vacation. On race day, I approached the race to do my best in the swim and bike and see what happens with the run. Having taken three weeks off, I thought my foot would be healed, and everything would be fine. I was wrong. I got through the swim, which is always my biggest fear and my weakest of the three disciplines. I did it in a respectable time, one hour and nineteen minutes for 2.4 miles. I admit there was a moment in the swim when I wanted to quit. In triathlon, you can raise your hand during the swim portion if you need assistance of any sort. They have people in kayaks and canoes looking for anyone in distress. At the start, there are two thousand people smashed in a small area waiting for the gun to go off. The start of the Ironman was different than any race I'd competed in previously. We had to tread water out a bit in the lake. Once the gun went off, it was every person

A SIMPLE SOUL

for themselves. The course was a two-loop course, so the chances of getting some space were slim. Lake Placid isn't very wide, so it seemed pretty congested. I started breast stroking because I didn't want to put my face in the water when I could barely move. People were kicking and hitting from every angle. After about two hundred yds, I panicked. I thought I couldn't do it.

My heart was racing, and I could barely breathe. There was no way I could breaststroke 2.4 miles. That's just too far to breaststroke! But I was afraid to put my head in the water. I was close to raising my hand to get rescued. However, I knew if I did that, the race was over for me. If a canoe or kayak pulls you or assists you in the swim, you're done. I told myself, *I did not spend $1,200 to quit!* You may be thinking I was an idiot to spend $1,200 to do this insane race in the first place. I had those same thoughts many times during training. Race registration is usually $600 for Ironman. Lake Placid fills up within hours of registration opening, and if you're not in line the day it opens, you're not getting in. The other way to get in is through their charity. You pay twice as much, but half the entry fee goes to charity. This is how I justified the cost. It was a once-in-a-lifetime experience too. So, in the midst of my panicking, I told myself that I didn't spend that money to quit. I put my head in the water and swam. It took me a few minutes before I settled in, but I was ok. Many people tried to swim over me, but I held my ground. I felt pretty strong in the swim. When my feet touched the sand after 2.4 miles, I had never felt so accomplished. I had done it! It was the same feeling I had after my first marathon. If only the race ended there.

The bike went well. Six hours and twenty minutes for 112 miles. Again, I was happy with my time. When I ran into the transition area after getting off the bike, I saw Karen. What a sight for sore eyes! We started running together, but by mile 4, I knew there was no way I could run another 22 more. I began limping and thought if it were only a couple miles out, I'd limp in but to try to limp 22 miles would almost certainly do further damage to my existing injury. It hit me that I had to drop out. I began to cry. I told Karen to make me proud and finish strong, which she did, but I felt such defeat as I stopped. DNF (did not finish) was something no racer wants to see by their name under the race results. Someone had told me that if you're injured,

A SIMPLE SOUL

as hard as it is to drop out, you don't want to do more damage. In such instances, therefore, DNF meant "Did Nothing Foolish." That was how I justified dropping out. Still, I cried myself to sleep that night, feeling like such a failure! I knew that many of my friends and family had tracked us and would see that I had not finished. At least I did nothing foolish either.

Spending the following week in Lake Placid vacationing with our families was harder than I thought it would be. Karen, of course, wanted to celebrate her accomplishment. I didn't want to be a downer and sulk in my defeat, so I did my best to put on a happy face. Inside, I wanted to go home and cry. I felt terrible for Karen because she had accomplished such a fantastic thing, and I couldn't give her the recognition and congratulations that she deserved. My ego was crushed, and I let it get in the way.

KIMBERLY COWHERD

I LEARNED MANY LESSONS FROM THE IRONMAN EXPERIENCE

1. GET BITTER OR GET BETTER

SINCE I DIDN'T FINISH, I was so motivated to pick another Ironman and attempt it again. As with the lessons I learned in basketball when one falls, what matters is how quickly one gets up again. I was determined to complete an Ironman, so I got up quickly!

 A SIMPLE SOUL

2. LIFE ISN'T FAIR, PLAIN, OR SIMPLE

AS MUCH AS I TRAINED and worked hard, some things are out of our control. I felt that it wasn't fair that I wasn't able to finish, but life isn't fair, and it's a tough pill to swallow. How many times in our lives have we said something was not fair? Chances are, we were right. However, when we fail, life gives us choices. We have the option of feeling sorry for ourselves, feeling angry at the world, or learning from what went wrong and moving on.

3. IT'S NOT ALL ABOUT ME

THIS WAS THE MOST CHALLENGING LESSON to learn. I realized that I took so much away from Karen's accomplishment because I couldn't put my ego aside. It took me a while before I could even apologize. Karen understood my pain about not finishing, but she was hurt that I wasn't the friend she needed to celebrate her success. It took me a while to understand how I had hurt her. I was so caught up in my emotions and what I felt about myself that I didn't consider her feelings. We had been friends for years at that point. My ego issues after the Ironman almost destroyed our relationship. I am blessed that she forgave me. She could have held on to the hurt that she felt. Instead, she allowed herself to forgive me, and from that, we both became even closer. It was a life lesson for both of us.

The following year Vito and I registered and trained for the Florida Ironman. This time I completed it! It felt amazing, crossing the line together with a time of twelve hours, thirty-two minutes. Every race I've done has been humbling for me, but that one meant so much more be-

cause of what I had been through the previous year. We need to have the bad runs or races to appreciate the good ones. The same is true in our non-athletic lives. We need to have bad days and bad experiences to enjoy and appreciate the good ones. We can't focus and dwell on those bad days or experiences, or it'll take away the positive experiences' joy. I've learned to view everything that happens as a lesson of one sort or another. When things get complicated, I consider where the lesson resides in the experience. I remind myself that everything is temporary—good and bad—so whatever is happening will pass. I challenge myself to learn the lesson and move on.

Vito and I continued racing and training throughout the following years while living in Connecticut. We both qualified and raced in the USAT National Championship for the triathlon. It was a humbling experience to compete against the best of the best throughout the country for age groupers.

In March 2015, Colin was offered a job at FOX Sports in Los Angeles, CA. It was another offer he couldn't refuse. He came to Vito and me, asking if we'd move also. He wouldn't take the job and work on the other side of the country without the kids. Colin had remarried as well, so the thought of all of us moving to LA for Colin to pursue his career might sound a little odd, but I understood his dilemma. Since my family still lived in Las Vegas, I suggested that we move to Vegas and Colin move to LA, and we would figure out how to make it work with the kids. It's only an hour flight between the two cities or a four-hour drive. We could make that work. So, that summer, we all moved.

I was thrilled to be back on the west coast, close to my family. Vito had wanted to move to a warmer climate for years, so it wasn't a difficult move for him either. He primarily worked from home with some travel here and there. Again, we said we'd find a way to make it work. Where there's a will, there's a way.

It was great to be back on the west coast, close to my family. Colin jumped right into his new television show in LA and the kids adjusted to the new environment. We moved, but our house in Connecticut was still on the market, so there was some added stress. As the months went by and there were no offers on our house, the tension built. Even though we were okay financially, carrying both mortgages and the pressure to sell our home took its toll on our marriage. Again, I looked at the financial crisis as temporary. In my view, it was only money, and we were okay. Unfortunately, Vito saw it differently. Some days he acted as if he had lost his best friend. Yes, we were losing money, but that's all we were losing. In life, as the saying goes, you win some, and you lose some. Real estate is no different. Not every real estate transaction is profitable. We had our health and each other, so in my mind, we were okay. I knew our house would eventually sell, and it did. It was on the market for almost a year before it sold.

Vito and I started going to therapy because I felt we were growing in different directions. The move required a more considerable adjustment for him than I had expected. I couldn't believe that a relationship that had been so strong at one time was falling apart. I began to feel guilty and ashamed for even considering dissolving this marriage. Vito had moved cross country with me and had been a significant part of my life for almost ten years at that point. When we were first married, I thought he was perfect for me. And he was. The dialogue in my head was so conflicting. What would people think? What would my family and his family think? Once again, looking in from the outside, ours looked like the perfect marriage. Vito adored me and gave me everything under the sun. We owned a beautiful, 5,000 square foot home on the golf course with a fantastic backyard featuring a pool with a waterfall and hot tub. We belonged to a country club, owned a Range Rover, a convertible Jeep, and a Cadillac. We took vacations every month, staying at the Four Seasons and dined at fine restaurants frequently. He bought me expensive jewelry and clothes. I had all the material things any woman would want. But deep in my heart, I was sad. Once again, I knew I couldn't stay in a marriage for the wrong reason. Although I cared deeply for him, I knew that we were moving in different directions. The emotions were again mixed. The mourning I felt for the loss of this relationship was unbearable, but I knew I had to move on.

 We divorced within months. It happened quickly, but I did not doubt that I was doing the right thing. Once again, I dealt with feelings of failing at another marriage. Along came the guilt and shame. Although I will say, going through the third divorce was a little bit easier. That may

# A SIMPLE SOUL

have been because I was older and knew some of the emotions to expect. I made the decision and did it quickly without as much self-doubt as on previous occasions. I still questioned myself and my character. I wondered if maybe I wasn't meant to be married. Perhaps I wasn't the marrying type. However, I believe in marriage. Somehow, though, I couldn't seem to get it right. I beat myself up about this for a long time. I knew being alone and raising my children would be the best thing for me. So, I packed up and started over—again.

KIMBERLY COWHERD

LESSONS LEARNED IN TRIATHLON

1. DON'T LOOK TOO FAR AHEAD

TRIATHLON TEACHES YOU TO FOCUS on the discipline (sport) you are doing at the time you're doing. It requires that you stay in the moment. When you are swimming, don't think about the bike. When you're biking, don't think about the run. When you're running, focus on one mile at a time. Breaking things down into manageable components and staying present in the moment helps our concentration and lets us guide our energy to where it's needed. Worrying is a waste of imagination—worrying amounts to wasting energy that we could use in our lives otherwise.

When I was a financial planner, I coached my clients to view their finances in a few ways. Enjoy today but save for tomorrow. You can't sacrifice everything hoping for a stable financial future. Still, you can't squander everything today and not plan for tomorrow. If you look too far

# A SIMPLE SOUL

ahead, you won't enjoy the moment. Be present today because we are not promised tomorrow. Every day is a gift. Assess the degree to which you may be looking too far ahead and worrying about what might happen. Question the extent to which you waste energy worrying about the future. Do your best to be present in the moment.

2. WORK ON YOUR STRENGTHS AS WELL AS YOUR WEAKNESSES

IT'S NATURAL TO WANT TO AVOID DOING what we aren't good at. Triathlon forces you to give each discipline appropriate attention in training. As I said, I was never a great swimmer, but triathlon forced me to do it, and by the end of my racing years, I developed into a decent swimmer. Triathlon forced me to look at more than one discipline or sport when my fitness activity consisted only of running at that time. Triathlon helped me develop into a better, well-rounded athlete. As in life, we can look at our weaknesses and avoid improving on them. Or we can dedicate energy and time to making ourselves more well-rounded. We can apply this approach to our professional, financial, personal, and family life. Consider the areas of life in which you are weaker or stronger—whether you spend sufficient amounts of time working on both weaknesses and strengths. Be particularly honest with yourself about whether you are avoiding developing areas in which you may be weaker than others.

 A SIMPLE SOUL

3. Everything is relative

Triathlon opened my eyes to the idea that everything is relative. When you are training, you gradually build from week to week. The training program I used for my athletes and myself included a steady progression for three straight weeks, followed by a drop. We repeated the pattern, and before we knew it, we had achieved our goal of preparedness for the triathlon. Say you are training for the run portion, and you have one long run per week. You may start running around 8 miles the first week, 10 miles in week two, 12 miles in week three, and then taper back to 8 miles for week four. Over the following three weeks, you increase to 14, then 16, then 18, followed by a taper back to 14. By the time you return to a 14 mile run, your mindset shifts to "oh, last week I ran 18. This week I am *only* running 14 miles." A carefully choreographed plan for conditioning allows us to compare our long runs relative to what we once considered long versus what we view as long runs as our training progresses. Once you are completing the 20 mile runs, 15 or 16 miles seem easy. It's all relative.

Many aspects of life are similar. Consider what or who we are comparing ourselves to in our daily lives. As an athlete, I was programmed to compete. My competition was whomever I was trying to beat. Thus, as long as I was better than they were, I felt like I won. However, in life, such comparisons can lead to a vicious cycle of never being good enough, having enough, or doing enough. Constantly remind yourself that you are on your own journey and live your own life. Stay in your lane. Reflect on how often you compare yourself to others. Consider if what you want in life is about keeping up with your neighbor or if you genuinely want something because it aligns with your own goals and objectives. To whose life are you comparing yours? Take time to reflect on how appreciative and grateful you are for what you have and assess how much time you spend thinking about what you do not have.

 A SIMPLE SOUL

4. THINK LIKE A BUMBLEBEE AND TRAIN LIKE A RACEHORSE

JOE FRIEL, THE AUTHOR of *The Triathlete's Training Bible,* advocates thinking like a bumblebee. In theory, a bumblebee shouldn't be able to fly. Scientists have researched how it's possible, and the consensus is that bumblebees should not be able to fly. The physics behind the research suggests that bumblebees' bodies are too big and heavy relative to their tiny wings. Apparently, no one told the bumblebee that it can't fly. So, it flies around fine. It flies because it believes it can.

As an athlete, it is helpful to adopt the same mentality. Believe that you can do anything despite evidence to the contrary. Do not let your past, family, peers, or competitors influence you to think otherwise. You have to have that mindset.

You also need to train like a racehorse. Racehorses train like athletes. They do intervals, lactate threshold training, wear heart rate monitors, and run the distance required to compete. They don't second guess if they have run enough to be prepared for race day. They have trainers, special diets, and they get nervous on race day, just like we do. However, they trust their training and run their own race on race day.

As athletes, we can easily overthink our training. We need to trust that the work we put into something will pay off. It's easy to have self-doubt. It takes courage to have faith in oneself. Triathlon has taught me this lesson, and it is one on which I continue to focus. Question if you have the work ethic necessary to achieve what you most desire in life. Do you trust the path you've chosen?

Most importantly, do you believe in yourself? Where do your doubts come from? What inspires you and sings to your soul?

 A SIMPLE SOUL

5. WE CAN ALWAYS CONTROL EFFORT AND ATTITUDE

MANY THINGS IN TRAINING and races are out of our control, such as the training program, race conditions, weather conditions, the others on the course, flat tires, or getting kicked during the swim. The two things we have 100% control over are our effort and attitude. Bearing that in mind will serve us well in all areas of our lives. Our effort is in our control. Are we giving whatever we are tackling 100%? Or are we quick to give up or quit? As long as we give whatever we are doing in life our best effort, that's all we can ask of ourselves, and that's all anyone can ask of us.

Controlling our attitude is somewhat different. We all know people who constantly look at the bright side, no matter what the situation. I love those people. They are diamonds in the rough. It's so easy to be negative and complain. It's easy to be lazy. Have you ever driven around a parking lot several times looking for a close spot instead of just parking in a far spot and walking to the store? We probably spend more time driving around looking for that close space than it would take to park farther away and walk. But it's easy to get lazy. Do we take the stairs if they are available or go to the escalator or elevator? I heard a comedian talk about people who get on escalators and stand. He says that you're supposed to keep walking; it's not a ride! I laughed at the image. A line of people just standing as the escalator carries them up. But it's true—keep moving, people!

Perhaps it is our instinct to be negative, like a survival skill. Maybe being negative as self-protection is natural. Still, we have to be mindful about when self-protection becomes a selfish act. It takes effort to be positive and look on the bright side. The bright side is usually there, although it may be harder to find it in some situations. Positivity is a choice, however. Life is full of choices. We choose what to think about and how to react to situations. My kids tell me often, "You're always positive." I remind them that being positive is work. Sometimes I don't want to be positive, but what's the alternative? No one likes Debbie Downers or Negative Nellies. I force myself to look for the bright side in any situation.

 A SIMPLE SOUL

Looking on the bright side also requires developing more faith and trust in the universe. I know that things will happen out of my control. Some things are not meant to be understood or make sense to us. We have to trust that they will happen for a reason. Not everything makes sense to us at that moment, but if we continue to keep our hearts open to allow the goodness in, everything will be okay. We can't allow the hard times to harden us. We can choose not to let that happen. As long as I wake up in the morning, I know I can handle whatever the day brings. Ask yourself if you show up every day in life ready to give100%. When you don't feel like doing something, do you show up giving 100%, nonetheless? Do you stay positive even when life is challenging? If not, what takes you away from your peace?

6. TAKE CARE OF THE TEMPLE

IF WE CONSIDER how we take care of ourselves, many of us may be surprised at how much we neglect ourselves. For a triathlete, nutrition and rest are as crucial to the training regime as the workouts themselves. Proper hydration is critical! The average person should consume half of their body weight in ounces of water per day. I weigh around 125 pounds. I require 62.5 ounces of water every day or roughly eight eight-ounce glasses. That doesn't account for whether I'm working out that day. I have to hydrate to replenish what I've sweated out. Do you drink the proper amount of water daily?

The benefits of water are often overlooked. Water is a significant source of energy. When our bodies are adequately hydrated, blood flows through veins and arteries more efficiently, reducing high blood pressure. Water can also eliminate and reduce the incidence of ulcers, gas, gastritis, acid reflux, and IBS. A well-hydrated body purges toxins and metabolic waste better. Hydrated skin looks better, and our internal organs function better as well.

 A SIMPLE SOUL

Nutrition is also a key factor. Weight loss is a billion-dollar industry, so obviously, it's something with which our society struggles. When you're training, you have to be mindful of how you are fueling your body. I'm not going to go in-depth on nutrition, but cutting back on sugar, processed food, empty calories in snacks, and soda is an excellent place to start! We have to look at our bodies as if they were cars. If we put the cheap gas in them, they will not run as smoothly as on the higher-octane gas. You don't have to be an athlete for this to apply either. Healthy eating will lead to healthy living. Once we start eating better and drinking more water, we may sleep better and feel healthier overall. Healthy habits have a snowball effect. Good choices lead to more of the same. But there is an adverse effect as well. When you're not eating well, you may not feel motivated to work out. Then, guilt and stress can build up, which compromises sleep quality, and you may end up with negative feelings about yourself. Bad choices may lead to more bad decisions. Beyond water intake and good nutrition, we also need to be mindful of our self-care in other areas such as mental, emotional, and spiritual health. Are you getting what you need in all

realms of your life? What and who are you allowing into your temple?

When I lived in Portland, I had a neighbor who was a fantastic role model. She was about ten years older, but she was in incredible shape. She ran, did yoga and Pilates, and took excellent care of herself. She would say, "my body is a temple, not a pup tent." She was mindful of what she ate and drank and how she lived her life. Consider whether you're treating your body like a temple or pup tent. Are you taking care of your body, mind, and spirit? Do you take care of yourself, so you're equipped to take care of others? In what ways do you nourish your body, mind, and soul?

A SIMPLE SOUL

7. YOU ARE STRONGER THAN YOU THINK

ALL MY RACING made me a stronger person physically. It also strengthened my spirit. It has given me the courage and strength to do things I never thought possible. We are all stronger than we think we are. Self-doubt jumps into our heads much faster than strength and courage assume occupancy. We sometimes give up before we even start. We doubt we have what it takes to get what we want. I am living proof that we can all be strong when we have to be. I am just an ordinary woman with limited athletic ability. But I believed and will continue to believe in myself. I have faith in my ability to get stronger internally.

If I had listened to that coach in high school who told me that I was too short and too slow to play basketball in college, I never would have pursued my goal to play in college. I would never have played basketball at all, and basketball led me to run, which led me to do a triathlon. All my accomplishments required a tremendous amount of strength, more mentally than physically. Eighty percent of exercise is mental. When things get more challenging, we do get stronger. Positive self-talk and believing in ourselves allow anything to be possible.

Think of the most challenging thing you have ever done. It might be physical, emotional, or intellectual. From where did you draw your strength to accomplish what you achieved? That strength is still there. When push comes to shove, we can find and use our strength. What's the alternative? Ask yourself, "Do I believe that I am strong? When things become challenging, where do you pull your strength from?

A SIMPLE SOUL

8. BE HUMBLE

HUMILITY IS ONE OF THE MOST POTENT and vital attributes of growth. Triathlon has taught me humility. I have been humbled many times through racing. When you put yourself out there, thinking you've prepared and done all that you can, possibly feeling confident, defeat can still be inevitable. So much of life is out of our control. That is humbling. So much in a race is out of our control. That is humbling. We can get a flat tire at any time, get passed, have goggles break, or lack hydration or nutrition. All these things can be out of our control and affect our performance. We think we are prepared, but the outcome isn't 100% in our hands. Arrogance is the opposite of humility. There is a fine line between confidence and arrogance. We all know incredibly arrogant people, thinking they are close to perfect with few weaknesses. Our weaknesses don't mean that we are weak. We are human. Being humble allows us to be human, and it makes room for growth in our lives. Humility invites us to aim for progress but not expect perfection.

KIMBERLY COWHERD

Research shows that humble people handle stress more effectively and report higher levels of physical and mental well-being. When we have a humble mindset, we don't let pride get in the way. Humility is an asset for self-improvement. We acknowledge that we are not perfect. Instead, we are life learners constantly growing. Consider whether you live life humbly. Are you always looking for ways to improve? Do you acknowledge your humanity and embrace your strengths as well as your weaknesses?

"Hitch your wagon to a star"
—Ralph Waldo Emerson

YOGA

Rodney Yee and his wife, Colleen Saidman Yee

Seane Corn

CHAPTER FOUR

YOGA

"Kindness is more important than wisdom, and the recognition of that is the beginning of wisdom"

—Theodore Isaac Rubin

One of the most effective practices in my life that helped me find simplicity has been yoga. I have been practicing yoga for over 20 years, and it has completely transformed my spiritual, physical, and mental wellbeing. Over the past four years, I've seen the most progression. Yoga has brought simplicity to my life, something my soul has been yearning for. It's made me more patient, accepting, forgiving, and compassionate. Four years ago, after going through my divorce to my second husband, I knew I wanted to live a different life. Both my first and second husbands were successful, driven men. In both marriages, I yearned for more. Money couldn't buy my happiness. I need to be happy and complete within. I knew driving the Escalade, living in a large home, belonging to a country club, and having a second home were terrific things. Still, I didn't want these material things to define who I was. It is true that "the more you get, the more you want." In our society, we are programmed from an early age to do well in school, to get a good job, so we can buy lots of stuff. Why? Why are we not taught to search our souls and find our authentic selves so we can prosper as productive citizens contributing to society? Our society focuses on the material things and our status of what we drive, the clothes we wear, how we look, how big our house is, how nice our vacations are. We can quickly begin to develop unhealthy relationships with money. We're constantly driving to make more, so we spend more, but we need to work more to fulfill our material needs.

One of the best books I've read during my soul-searching years is Lynne Twist's *The Soul of Money*. She talks about the relationship we have with money. Is it a healthy

relationship? Many people think more is better or there just isn't enough. But when we focus on what's missing, we don't appreciate what we have. She makes a wonderful point that what we appreciate appreciates. Unfortunately, many people accumulate and accumulate, and still, they feel like they don't have enough. They live in a world of scarcity, worrying that they will never have enough. When is enough enough?

Many people go through their lives thinking if I had a little more, I'd be happy. Then they get it, and they say, again, if I just had a little more. The more people make, the more they want. It's the American dream, right? Big house, a job that pays well, vacations, expensive cars, etc. There is a saying in the financial world, "Pigs get fat, hogs get slaughtered." Greed and fear are the two things that drive the stock market. Greed is a terrible thing, but it's a subtle push in our society. There is merit in assessing how we use our money. Do we use it to help others? *The Soul of Money* was a fabulous read that opened my eyes to my relationship with money and how others may view it. Is money power and control or safety and stability? Is

it more powerful than God? Do we, in essence, "lose our souls" in the pursuit of money?

    I wanted to let go of all the "stuff" and simplify my life. With simplicity comes balance. I wanted to prove to myself that I didn't need possessions to make me who I am. Deep in my heart, the material things didn't matter. So, I moved out of our 5,000 sq ft home on the golf course, which I loved. It was built to look like an Italian villa with a courtyard, waterfalls, palm trees, and a magnificent backyard with a swimming pool and hot tub with waterfalls in both. I left all the furniture, took my personal belongings and my children, and moved into a modest 1,700 sq ft townhouse. I downsized my car and began to embrace living a simple lifestyle—no more fine dining and vacations every month.

    I analyzed how easy it was to walk away from all the material things and how liberated it made me feel. Although I was terrified to be on my own, I knew I'd be ok. I couldn't let fear keep me in a situation that wasn't good for my spiritual growth. Being raised Catholic but not practicing the religion, I felt that I needed to connect more with my spirituality. I had lost my connection to a

more spiritual life. There was more to me than my earthly possessions. I chose to be free of the clutter, physically and emotionally. I wanted to reconnect with my authentic self, my true self, my simple soul.

    I spent the next few years reflecting and developing a relationship with not only myself but with something more significant. I made a conscious choice not to be in a relationship. I had spent the last twenty-five years of my life in two different relationships, going from one to the other with not much time in between. I was a different person in my mid-forties than I was in my mid 20's when I married the first time. I needed to spend time with myself, no distractions, and just raise my children and plan my future. Being alone can be scary, but I looked at it as a time to do things for myself. Not being selfish here, but for once, not having to compromise on anything. I will say I enjoy it. Being the captain of my ship, sailing wherever the wind takes me. I had my children to raise, so it's not like it was all that fabulous, but the freedom I felt to be me was incredible. I needed that time for myself, but I also needed to develop a relationship beyond myself. I hesitate to use the word God because God can mean something different for everyone. It's not the God I was raised with as a Catholic. I think of God now as simply "goodness."

During that time, a close friend of the family, Sister Karen, told me about *Super Soul Sunday* on the Oprah Winfrey Network (OWN). Every Sunday morning, it is a one-hour show that features a guest discussing topics on a soulful level. Most guests are authors, but she's had actors, politicians, musicians, people of religion, entertainers, etc. I discovered this show years ago and have watched almost every episode since. It's like hitting the reset button every Sunday for my soul. I told my mom about it, and now she's hooked. We'll watch the show and then call each other after to discuss it. It's our book club.

Although I don't practice the Catholic religion anymore, spirituality has taken an important seat in my life. The show has opened my heart and mind to so much! I have read almost all of the books written by the authors who have been on the show. It has inspired me to pursue a life of goodness. It has opened me to different ways of living a spiritual life through mindfulness. I know that is what I was missing. That connection and relationship to

 A SIMPLE SOUL

the goodness of this world. Who knows, maybe Oprah will read this book and have me as a guest on her show. We do have something in common—we both ran a marathon. Just throwing it out to the universe. By the way, I can already envision what I will be wearing. Tune in!

I now have the most fantastic relationship with the goodness of this universe, and it has blessed me with more than I can imagine. Not materially, but deep within my soul. I feel such success in my life, and it isn't tied in any way to the material things in my life. It's about creating peace, serenity, and calmness in my heart. Creating an authentic self, not ego-driven. Honestly, I don't miss any of my previous lifestyles. There were times I almost felt gluttonous. Did I not deserve all these things? Or was it that all these things weren't what life is all about. Looking back, I feel some of it was for show.

When I lived in Connecticut, I was a Lululemon ambassador. If you're not familiar with Lululemon, they are a Canadian apparel company that sells expensive yoga pants. They have excellent workout apparel and have become extremely popular in the yoga community. They have running and other workout clothing for both men and women. When they opened a store in West Hartford, where I was living, they looked for five ambassadors to represent the company, ranging from yoga to spinning to running. A few of the employees went around town taking different instructor classes. They choose five local instructors to be ambassadors for the brand. I was honored that they chose me. I was their running ambassador. I had to do a photoshoot so they could put the gigantic photograph of me running up on the wall in the store. They chose a hot, humid day in June to do the photoshoot. They outfitted me, and we went to The Reservoir, a beautiful, picturesque backdrop for running. Trails and paths were lined with beautiful green trees and bodies of water. After about ninety minutes of running fifty yds then turning around to run back, running another fifty yards, and turning around to run back, my make-up was down my face, and I was just a hot mess. I must have run five miles in that period! Thank God they picked a shot at the beginning of the session where my make-up was where it was supposed to be, not down my face.

After a few months of being an ambassador, they chose one of us to go on a weekend self-help-type retreat

# A SIMPLE SOUL

in New York City, all expenses paid. I was honored that they chose me, and I jumped at the opportunity. I thought to myself that they picked me for one of two reasons.

1. I must need this or
2. I'm the most open-minded and will embrace this retreat and gain the most from it. I'm going with the second reason!

We weren't allowed to take notes in the sessions. It was a two-day retreat starting on Saturday at 7 am and ending at 10 pm, with one thirty-minute lunch break and a one-hour dinner break. The next day we started again at 7 am but only went to 7 pm. Needless to say, there was a tremendous amount of information, but one of the points that stuck with me was this. The instructor asked what motivates people. Many answers were shouted out...money, fear, power, etc. He explained that people are motivated for one of two reasons:

1. Trying to "look good."
2. Trying to avoid "looking bad."

I did a lot of thinking about that, and there is so much truth to it. Whether we realize it or not, we are concerned about what people think and, therefore, decide based on those motives. You've heard the saying, "Dance like nobody's watching." How would we live our lives if we thought that no one was watching? What if no one cared what we drove, what clothes we wore, or how big our house was? I'm not saying all of our choices and decisions are based on what others say or think, but if you reflect on some of your decisions and choices, how many have been the product of your authentic self? What do we genuinely want? Do our wants feed our ego? What do we truly need? Do these needs feed our ego? Does our ego need to be fed to avoid some pain we are feeling inside?

During the next few years by myself, I began practicing and teaching more yoga. My yoga journey has been fascinating. It started in my twenties when I was an avid runner. Feeling tight all of the time, I knew I needed to stretch more. I bought a VHS tape titled *Yoga for Athletes* by Rodney Yee. I didn't know much about yoga at the time. Whenever yoga was mentioned in conversation, I thought of chanting and meditating, neither of which I had time for at that point in my life. I just needed a good stretch. So, he was the first yoga instructor I had, and it was great. Lots

of stretching, no chanting or meditation. It was perfect. I did it at home after my runs, and Rodney had such a gentle way about him in his voice and the way he moved. I thought, "Wow, this yoga stuff makes you slow down and relax." The practice was something I wasn't used to and something that didn't come naturally to me. He was a fit, strong man doing impressive postures, and he did them in ways that were mindful and intentional. I was hooked!

Shortly after, I went to my first yoga studio in Portland, Oregon. It was Bikram Yoga, which again meant I was going to get a good stretch. Little did I know that it was a ninety-minute class in a one hundred and four-degree room. There are twenty-six postures that you do twice, holding the pose for one minute the first time and thirty seconds the next. It's a combination of standing and on the mat postures with two breathing exercises, one at the beginning and one at the end. Quite intense, but I loved it. That was my introduction to yoga. It kicked my ass. That's my kind of yoga. During the subsequent years, I tried different yoga types such as Hatha, Restorative, and Yin. Some I liked, some I didn't like as much, but again, doing yoga once or twice a week was what I needed, given all the running I was doing. It wasn't until I moved to Connecticut and began training for triathlon that I started teaching yoga.

I started teaching yoga at the gym where I was teaching spin, so it was an introductory yoga class. I did Bikram and other types of yoga at different studios in town. I started to embrace all the benefits that yoga provides physically. Besides "stretching," I found the internal benefits to be just as advantageous. All the twisting is great for our internal organs and flexibility in our spine. Yoga can help reduce stress and anxiety, restore hormonal balance, calm the nervous system, support the immune system, lower cortisol levels, the hormone released in response to stress, lower blood pressure, improve focus and concentration, and help you think clearly.

One year, I saw that Seane Corn was going to be a guest instructor at one of the studios I was going to, West Hartford Yoga. Seane Corn is a very well-known instructor in the yoga world. At that time, I got my monthly subscription to Yoga Journal, and Seane Corn was often on the cover. She's lovely. She has the most unique, gorgeous, long, curly hair I have ever seen. She's from LA and very respected in the yoga community. Of course, I had to go to her class when she was in town. That class changed how I looked at yoga! It wasn't just a physical thing anymore. Sean spoke on such a spiritual level that I left feeling like a light bulb had gone off in my head. She shared some personal experiences, and then I knew that yoga had saved her. Just like basketball, running, and triathlon had saved me during times in my life, yoga had been her savior.

One year ago, I was researching yoga retreats. I had always wanted to go to one, so I decided to treat myself. I was looking for a location not too far from Las Vegas, where I live. One of the first ones I came across was in San Jose, California. I looked up the guest instructors, and Seane Corn and Rodney Yee were among them. I couldn't believe it. Rodney Yee was my first introduction to yoga, and Seane Corn brought another level to my yoga practice. They were both going to be at the retreat. It was meant to be! I immediately booked it! After booking my retreat, I had to pick what classes I wanted to attend. Of course, I wanted to do as many as possible, but some overlapped others, so it was a little tricky making sure I could do the ones I wanted. After signing up for about five of Sean's classes and two of Rodney's, I thought Seane might think I was stalking her, so I took fewer classes with her and some with other instructors who I didn't know. It was only a weekend retreat, but after four classes on the first day, I could barely move for day two. I couldn't believe how sore I was. But I wanted to absorb as much as I could from as many instructors as possible.

The weekend started with Seane Corn as the keynote speaker welcoming us to the retreat. She talked about her new book, *Evolution of the Soul*. She expressed her concern over writing a book and how it took her years to overcome her fear. I knew that speech was meant for me to hear. I've had writing a book on my bucket list for almost thirty years, so I knew it was time. What was holding me back? Fear that I'm not a writer. Well, that was one among many other worries. Everything she said resonated with me. I am so grateful that her message motivated me to get over the excuses for not writing my book. I'm not a writer by trade, but I definitely have something to say. She did it, so why couldn't I? I took from her speech that we are all the same, filled with fear and love. She had

A SIMPLE SOUL

a message to share, and she followed her heart, moved past her fear of writing, and was there talking about her book. I was meant to be there, at that moment, hearing her speak. She motivated me just like I hope my book motivates you. It was a fantastic retreat!

Yoga provides me with connections to mind, body, and soul, which were life-changing for me. Yoga started as something strictly for physical purposes. Still, as the years went on, different layers of my practice were opened. Just like an onion, once you peel the top layer off, you see the numerous layers underneath. I wanted to get down to the core. I began to develop a strong sense of spirituality and began healing my soul. I read numerous self-help books, which helped me understand that life's journey is not a destination. I started practicing kindness toward myself. I read several books by Brene Brown that helped in my healing process. One of my favorites by her is *The Gift of Imperfections*. I have always been tough on myself and on the people close to me too. My expectations of others may have been unrealistic. Learning to embrace my imperfections has given me the empathy to accept other people's imperfections as well as my own. I look back and realize how much of my life was unconsciously spent on living to make other people happy. So, I began listening more to my inner voice. But even more importantly, I started trusting that inner voice. Many of us don't stop and listen to what our hearts and souls are saying and what they need.

In stillness, we can hear so much. Beyond listening to myself, I've learned to trust myself and that all these life events happened for a reason. They made me the person I am today. Knowing that the universe has a great plan for me, I trust that in the end, everything will be ok. It has been a shift for me to move from fear and the unknown to trust and love. I look at all the experiences I've had, and it's easy to let the good ones fill our hearts with love. The challenge is not letting the bad experiences or hard times harden our hearts and souls. I love the saying, "get bitter or get better." Yoga taught me to be kinder to myself. Stillness and reflection have also been gifts I received from yoga. Stillness allows us to be quiet and truly "listen." I believe that if more people took time to pause and reflect, they would find more inner peace. It allows us to heal. Heal the soul, body, and mind. It brings a sense of

 A SIMPLE SOUL

calmness to our hearts. It brings mindfulness to our lives. Every day I choose to live present to what life brings to me and what I allow into my thoughts and heart; I create a world of inner peace. I understand that life will bring us challenges and struggles. Still, it's how we allow those adverse circumstances to affect us. Do we break down, refusing to get up, or do we break down but rise strongly? I choose to rise strongly!

Yoga hasn't just provided me with a more peaceful sense of myself. It has also allowed my body and soul to heal. We are all broken. Remember that. We are all on our own journey. Suppose we understand that everyone's journey is different and that we are all doing the best we can with what we have. In that case, we can move through life with more compassion and empathy.

One of the most powerful experiences I had while teaching yoga was at the end of a class. I taught a 5:30 am yoga class on Tuesdays and Thursdays at a gym a few miles away. My alarm would go off at 5 am; I'd have a few sips of coffee, get dressed, brush my teeth, and be out the door by 5:15 am. I gave those students so much credit for getting there at that hour to practice yoga. Living in Las

Vegas, I had many people getting off work and coming to yoga before they went home to go to bed. Vegas is a 24-hour town, literally, so I had casino dealers, construction workers, you name it in my class. All of them were there for a different reason.

One Tuesday morning, I noticed a man in my class, Joseph. He had taken my spin class before, but he wasn't a regular group class participant. He'd show up from time to time. Cardio wasn't his thing. He was the bodybuilding type. Joseph was about six feet tall and built of solid muscle. He was covered with tattoos from head to toe. If I were to come across Joseph in a dark alley, I might be scared, but he was a very gentle soul; I could tell.

I said good morning to him, somewhat surprised that he was doing yoga. He had never been to one of my classes, especially a 5:30 am class. Class began, and I noticed that Joseph's body wasn't used to the practice as we moved through postures. Given that he's all muscle, and a lot of it, some of the poses seemed challenging for him. But he did what he could do. I usually end my classes with a quick message after some deep breaths with our eyes closed. It's usually something along these

 A SIMPLE SOUL

lines— "Let's take a moment to honor what we've done, who we are, and all that we have. Keep this feeling of love and light in your hearts and carry it with you throughout your day. Your soul is perfect the way it is. Our egos get in the way. Use your gifts and talents and spread your love and light to others. Take this strength and courage and move today with integrity and honesty. Have a beautiful Tuesday. Namaste."

    I change the rhetoric from day to day, but that's generally the message I like to leave people with. As I stood up to collect the candles through the room and turn the lights back on, Joseph stood up too. I walked over to him. He had tears in his eyes. I went to hug him, and he embraced me so tightly and began to sob. I didn't say a word. I just held him. It felt like a long time, but I'm sure it was only 30 seconds or so. Not knowing what to say, I didn't say a word. When he let go, he looked at me and said, "Thank you!" He shared that he was a recovering addict, and that morning he had hit rock bottom. At 4 am he went to the ATM and withdrew five hundred dollars. He was going to get his fix, but he knew he shouldn't. Instead, he went home and went online to see what classes were available at the gym. His choice was spinning or yoga. He chose yoga. He had never done it, but he said it was what he needed. There was a reason he was there. He couldn't thank me enough. It was such a humbling experience for both of us. I was going to teach yoga, but Joseph needed something much more profound than a class. At that moment, I felt so blessed that I could help him, even if it was only for the moment.

Yoga taught me two things that I will continue to work on both externally and internally. They are balance and flexibility. Physically, as we age, these are the first skills we lose unless we practice them regularly. I teach group classes a few days a week at a fifty-five and older community. We do chair yoga every week, and toward the end of class, I have them stand and work on balance postures. As we age, recovering from a broken hip or fall can be devastating. If we can prevent falls by working on our balance and strengthening our feet and ankles, we are less likely to fall. If people do not fall, they are less likely to break a hip.

Developing physical balance is imperative, but it is equally important to maintain balance in our lives. I

 A SIMPLE SOUL

learned that through the myriad adventures I've been blessed to experience. Balance is a common denominator in many areas of a well-lived life. Yoga has taught me to balance my mind, body, and soul. Flexibility is as important as balance. A body in motion stays in motion. We have to keep moving physically, or our mobility will be seriously impaired. I can tell which of my elderly students are active in their daily routines. They move better, are in less pain, and tend to look younger. Their spirits are more alive, as well.

We must also keep our minds adaptable and flexible. I have read that the most successful people also tend to be among the most flexible. They are willing and able to change with the demands of the environment. When I feel stuck in my ways, I question whether there are other ways of thinking or doing something. I consider if I'm stuck in a comfort zone. That leads me to ponder what frightens me about change or settling into a less-comfortable space or routine. These days, we have to be willing to change and adapt to our environment more than ever. With advancements in technology, medicine, and other areas, it is more

KIMBERLY COWHERD

urgent than ever to be flexible and open to learning and growing as the world around us changes.

*"Life isn't about finding yourself.
Life is about creating yourself."*

—George Bernard Shaw

CHAPTER FIVE

MANIFESTING

"What we see depends mainly on what we look for"

—John Lubbock

J am a huge believer in manifesting. I think I was doing it from an early age, not knowing the impact it could have. Manifestation is the idea that something becomes real through visualization and believing that it'll happen. In religion, we pray. We ask God for many things. I used to engage in traditional prayer, but even that has evolved as well. I still engage in the form of prayer, but instead of asking God for something, I thank him. My prayers have become a one-way conversation with God about gratitude and thankfulness. I don't ask God for anything anymore because I have faith and trust that whatever is meant to be will be. I offer my requests through prayer to the universe in keeping with the principles of manifestation.

My belief in manifestation began with visualization practices when I played basketball. I would picture the ball going through the hoop immediately after I released it. I would do this on every free throw. As I walked up to the line, I would picture the ball going in. Then I'd be handed the ball, and I'd shoot. I was a very consistent free throw shooter, and visualization was a factor in my success. As a kid, visualization was all I knew; I did not know about manifesting. As I aged, I understood the importance of putting out positive energy. I believe that energy may start out as neutral, but eventually, it is either negative or positive. Think of running water. Water that doesn't move becomes stagnant and stale, which is a negative state. The same is true of energy. If we stay neutral too long, our energy will stagnate. Our energy has a lot to do with our state of mind and our perception of the world around us, and our role in our experiences. There is always more than one way to look at something. When we focus on the negative, our energy becomes negative.

A SIMPLE SOUL

I believe in karma, too. What we put out into the universe comes back to us. Our minds are powerful, and if we think we can accomplish something, we can. When we manifest, we put our thoughts, visions, and beliefs out to the universe and visualize them coming to fruition. The following is an example of an amazing manifestation in my life.

In 2014, Vito, husband number two, gave me tickets to the Ellen show as a Christmas gift. I love Ellen! Her positivity and generosity are inspiring. I always watched her show while I cooked dinner. My husband knew how much I loved her, so he got tickets for him and me to go. That was one of the best Christmas presents ever. In March, we flew from Hartford, Connecticut, to Las Vegas, Nevada, to drop my kids with their grandparents. The next day Vito and I took off for LA. The show for which we had tickets was the following day, but Vito had some business to attend to with his LA clients. That morning, I went hiking through Runyon Canyon Park. I mapped out about a six-mile hike. The base of the trail was about a mile, so I planned to hike a couple of miles, turn around, and head back to the hotel to shower and go to the show.

As I began my walk, I had a feeling that something good was going to happen. I already knew I was going to the Ellen show, so that was obviously good. As I got to the base of the trail, I saw many hikers and runners. I started up the trail. Shortly after that, I encountered two men walking with their dogs. I started chit-chatting with them, and before I knew it, I was already almost to my turnaround point.

During our conversation, I told them I was visiting LA and going to the Ellen show that afternoon. They loved Ellen, too, so they were extremely excited for me. I also told them that I wasn't just going to the show but that I might be on the show. They looked at me, a little confused. I said that if there is a skit, which was a possibility, I would be picked to be a contestant. I just had a feeling. I could see myself being chosen to participate. I threw my vision out to the universe by verbalizing my intentions, and the universe responded! I turned shortly after to head back to the hotel and said my goodbyes to my new friends. I told them to watch Ellen because they might just see me. I think they thought I was crazy. They just laughed and kept going.

 A SIMPLE SOUL

After I returned to the hotel, I showered, and Vito met me at the hotel. I wore the most colorful outfit I could find. I heard Ellen likes bright colors, so my sunshine yellow pants were perfect! We then arrived at the Ellen show. The audience gathered in the parking lot before entering the building. After a few minutes, two producers came out and announced what would happen when we entered the building and found our seats. They also announced that there "might" be a skit. They said they would walk around and see if any audience members liked 80s and 90s music. At that point, I knew they would pick me! As one producer walked near the section of the crowd I was in, she asked, "does anyone here like 80s and 90s pop?" I jumped on that one. I raised my hand and said I was a spin instructor, and that's all I play in my class. I love that music. She liked that answer and told me to stand in a different part of the parking lot. There were around forty people in the group, and they asked each of us where we were from, what we did, etc. I could tell that they were getting us to talk so they could assess our personalities. I made sure they knew how energetic and enthusiastic I was about being at the show. Then they told about half

of us to go to a different part of the parking lot, and the others went back to the main crowd.

At this point, I was separated from Vito. Once the group was narrowed down to about twenty, I thought that my odds were getting better. They came around one more time, asking more questions and narrowing the crowd further. They told twelve of us to go into a trailer that was parked outside of the parking lot. We went in and took seats. I looked around and knew that if they were choosing people for a skit, I was the best candidate in the group; not the oldest, not the youngest, but I had the most energy. A few producers asked each of us our name, occupation, and where we were from. As I'd told them earlier, I repeated that I was a spin and yoga instructor, a women's high school basketball coach, and a triathlon coach. I think I may have impressed the producer with my activity level. Usually, Ellen's skits involve two or three participants, so my odds of being chosen were pretty good. After they gave us instructions for entering the building, we were told to find the person with whom we'd come because they'd already been seated. I went through security and came out at the back of the studio, so all the audience members had their backs to us. I looked for Vito, hoping he was sitting at the end of an aisle. He was seated right in the middle of a row halfway up from the front. I made my way through the crowd and sat next to him. Most of the people were up dancing while the music played. Within a few minutes, I saw producers going up and down the aisles, looking. One made eye contact with me and gestured with his finger to come. I got up, and he told Vito and me to sit in seats at the end of an aisle. YES! I knew they were going to pick me! I could feel the adrenaline rush as it does before a game or race.

The show started, and within the first half-hour, Ellen did a skit. She had Randy Jackson on as a guest. The skit was Humdinger. Randy wore headphones and would hum a song from the 90s that was playing in his headphones. She had three contestants playing, and they had to buzz and guess the song. When it was time to call the contestants to the front, Ellen said, "Can I have Kim Iacovazzi...." and the rest of the sentence was a blur. I jumped up, sprinted to the stage, gave both Ellen and Randy a hug, and strategically placed myself in the middle of the other two contestants. Being on stage with the bright lights and my heart racing, I'm surprised I even remembered my name. I was SO nervous. My vision had manifested. I made a complete idiot of myself, but it was an incredible experience. You can look up the episode on YouTube and see what a fool I made of myself, but it was a blast!

To this day, I continue to manifest. I ask myself what I want, I visualize it happening, and what it would feel like if my vision manifested. I verbalize my vision so the universe hears it. I know if I live life with integrity and courage, the universe will reward me. If I continue to do things for the right reasons, with intention and mindfulness, I will receive all the blessings I need. I have moved away from the world's material wants. I ask the universe for deeper connections among myself and others. I am blessed every day to open my eyes and start the day knowing that goodness is out there, in everything. Do we take the time to see it? Do we try to add to it? Do we make conscious efforts every day to nourish our souls? Do we make conscious choices to nourish our bodies and our minds? Life is a gift. We all have the same twenty-four hours each

day. Do we choose to live every day with gratitude and appreciation?

These are questions I hope you ask yourself. Listen to your answers. As with anything we do, we can't do it once and expect change. We have to make desirable practices part of our daily lives. Take time every day to reflect, nourish, appreciate, and honor what life brings us. It's easy to go through the motions of life, losing our sense of purpose and ourselves eventually. All the events in my life have made me stronger, more courageous, more compassionate, and more empathetic. I look at the world as a giant classroom. We are all students, showing up every day for our lesson. Some lessons are harder to learn, but we will grow and thrive as long as we are lifelong students.

"There is in each of us so much goodness that if we could see its glow, it would light the world."

—*Sam Friend*

CHAPTER SIX

SPRING CLEANING

"Accept yourself, love yourself, and keep moving forward. If you want to fly, you have to give up what weighs you down." —Roy T. Bennett

If you have never done spring cleaning, you need to start. Ideally, springtime is a great time to start fresh by getting rid of the clutter in your house. Discard things you don't use or don't have a purpose for anymore. As a society, we accumulate way too much stuff. I have moved several times, and each time I move, I go through my things and ask myself, "Do I need this?" If I haven't used it in the previous six months, the answer is probably no. However, we accumulate things and create attachments to them. Before you know it, your house is full of stuff you don't need. I'm not saying to get rid of all

A SIMPLE SOUL

your possessions but be mindful of the attachments you have to these things. Ask yourself, "Is this something I need? Or does it add value to my life?"

Every time I move, I am forced to do spring cleaning. The less I have, the less I have to move, which I do myself except for the heavy furniture. But I love the feeling of paring down. I think I need to move every few years for that reason! However, moving isn't fun, and I know that's not the answer, so I consciously declutter every six months. I am amazed by how much I donate when I go through all my closets, drawers, garage, and bedrooms. Packing up these things and taking them to a local donation center is exhilarating. The feeling of letting go of the clutter can be liberating. It is hard to let some things go, but if it's been in a closet for six months, how much will you miss it? Does it add value to your life? Again, the answer is probably no, so let it go! Not only are we getting rid of the excess baggage, but we are opening our space. Rooms look bigger and less congested. Rooms look cleaner, more accessible, and more open.

What if we did spring cleaning in our lives too? What if we let go of what's not adding value or serving a purpose in our lives? We can apply this notion to many areas of our life. Think of our minds. What negative thought processes do we carry that aren't serving a purpose or adding value? Let them go! We can spring clean regularly, personally, professionally, and in relationships. I have found that in stillness or reflection, I can access what is and is not working in my life. I do some form of meditation every day, but not in the conventional way many think of meditating. For me, meditation ranges from a few minutes to an hour. I've engaged in many forms of meditation. When I ran, I used that time to be with my thoughts—no music, just my breath. I think that is why I enjoyed running alone so much. It was my time to think. Spinning also provides me with the time to think and let go of so much that I'm inclined to hold on to.

In yoga, the final posture is called Savasana, dead man's pose, or corpse pose. In the posture, you lay completely still. Some people find being still uncomfortable. People tend to fidget. Staying still involves resisting any urges to fidget or move. That's only the first part. The second part is learning to remain completely still in your mind, letting go of all your thoughts, focusing on the

breath, and ultimately surrendering. That is true stillness. Depending on the practice or type of class you take, it can be five to ten minutes. Usually, the pose is the best five or ten minutes of my day. Its effects are indescribable. To surrender and let go is healing. Stillness forces us to be vulnerable, which in turn allows us to soften our hearts and souls. It allows us to restore our courage and inner strength. It will enable us to reset. In these ways, being still is like spring cleaning for the soul. It took me years before I understood what stillness of the mind meant and the benefits of doing it.

I recently purchased an infrared sauna. I read about the benefits of infrared light for the body, and I was sold. Infrared light helps cells regenerate or repair themselves. It improves the circulation of oxygen-rich blood in the body, improving faster healing of deep tissues and relieving pain and inflammation. It reduces stress and anxiety, reduces muscle fatigue, detoxification, helps collagen production, and helps with scars and wrinkles. I've been using mine every day since I bought it a month ago. I use it anywhere from twenty to forty-five minutes per day. I

put on some soulful, easy listening music, close my eyes, and surrender. I focus on my breath and quiet my mind.

I have been practicing yoga for over twenty years now. I'll admit, for the first few years of yoga, I thought Savasana was a complete waste of time. I don't have time to just lie there. I had to go run errands, pay bills, cook dinner and do everything else that piles up in a day. It took me years to master the stillness of the mind. Even today, I catch my mind wandering and have to pull it back. Now I am aware of when I'm losing focus or stillness. I can say that it helped me connect more deeply to myself, to others, and most importantly, to the universe. It's in our stillness that we find the answers for which we are looking. We become in tune with what's in our hearts and what our souls are telling us.

Stillness or meditation is like daily spring cleaning for me. Taking time to do some spring cleaning internally and externally in your environment helps get rid of the clutter. The key is not to add more clutter to our space because we have created space. Instead, the point is to live with that new space and see if it's necessary to add anything more to it. The answer is probably no. Less is more.

A SIMPLE SOUL

I have performed a spring-cleaning process with every house I moved into. I sold and/or donated almost everything I had and started over. I usually kept clothes and the essential kitchen things but bought only what I needed. It's incredible how much crap we have and accumulate daily. I even chose a color palette that invited peacefulness to my space. My primary colors are neutral—grey, black, and white, and I have splashed green throughout. Green is the fourth chakra, the heart chakra. I chose this color because it represents balance, calmness, and serenity, all the qualities that I wanted to define my environment.

Some people find stillness in prayer or going to church. Some find it in meditation. It doesn't have to be daily. Weekly, monthly even annually is better than nothing. But the more you pray, the more you discover a better version of yourself. It doesn't matter what form you find it in, just find it! Spring-clean your house and your soul!

I have no idea what the next chapter or decade will look like in my life. I do know that I am prepared to embrace whatever this world has to offer with open arms! The good, the bad, the sorrow, the joy. It's all inevitable, and it's ahead of me. I don't want to avoid pain and suffering. I want to feel it, let it pass, and move on from it even stronger. Everything that happened and all my emotions from my life experiences have brought me where I am now. So, I share with you my story. You have a story too. Neither yours nor mine is better or worse than the other; they are different. We all can learn from each other. We can choose how we move in life. Will we move toward fear and away from love or toward love and away from fear? Fear is just an emotion; it doesn't define us. It doesn't become real unless we allow it. Choose love, kindness, empathy, compassion, and trust not only for yourself but for others as well. Ask yourself, "How simple is my life? How simple is my soul?"

"Cry. Forgive. Learn. Move on. Let your tears water the seeds of your future happiness."

—Steve Maraboli

CHAPTER SEVEN

QUOTES AND BOOKS

MY FAVORITE QUOTES:

"We make a living by what we get, but we make a life by what we give."

—Winston Churchill

"Look for what is good, and you will find it."

—Anne Perry

"At least once a day, allow yourself the freedom to think and dream for yourself."

—Albert Einstein

"You are far from the end of your journey. The way is not in the sky. The way is in the heart."

—Buddha

"The more you take, the less you have."

—Kung Fu Panda

"When we know better, we do better."

—Maya Angelou

"We can't be afraid of change. You may feel very secure in the pond that you are in, but if you never venture out of it, you will never know that there is such a thing as an ocean, a sea. Holding onto something good for you; now may be the very reason why you don't have something better."

—C. Joybell C.

 A SIMPLE SOUL

"We find what we search for, or if we don't find it, we become it."

—Jessamyn West

"Only passions, great passions, can elevate the soul to great things."

—Denis Diderot

"There are two ways of spreading light; to be the candle or the mirror that reflects it."

—Edith Wharton

"They can because they think they can."

—Virgil

"Beginnings are usually scary, and endings are usually sad, but it's everything in between that makes it all worth living."

—Bob Marley

"What you are will show in what you do."

—Thomas Edison

"Life is a journey to be experienced, not a problem to be solved."

—Winnie the Pooh

"She doesn't use her love to make him weak. She uses love to keep him strong."

—Stevie Wonder, "That Girl"

A SIMPLE SOUL

"Just keep swimming, swimming, swimming...."

—Dory in Finding Nemo

"I've learned that people will forget what you said, will forget what you did, but people will never forget how you made them feel."

—Maya Angelou

"If you do not hope, you will not find what is beyond your hopes."

—St. Clement

"Action is eloquence."

—William Shakespeare

KIMBERLY COWHERD

"Act as if what you do makes a difference. It does."

—William James

"I believe in the power of dreams. I can be anything, go anywhere."

—Desree

"Expectation kills. Just go with the flow; you might be surprised when something better comes along in an unexpected way."

—Joyram Shaw

SOME OF MY FAVORITE BOOKS

Daring Greatly by Brene Brown

Breaking the Habit of Being Yourself
    by Dr. Joe Dispenzo

Rising Strong by Brene Brown

The Five Love Languages by Gary Chapman

The Millionaire Next Door
    by Thomas J Stanley and William D. Danko

The Seven Habits of Highly Effective People
    by Stephen Covey

Lean In by Sheryl Sandberg

What on Earth Am I Here For? by Rick Warren

Brave Enough by Cheryl Strayed

Anatomy of the Spirit by Caroline Myss

The Soul of Money by Lynne Twist

The Gratitude Diaries by Janice Kaplan

Oola: Finding Balance in an Unbalanced World
    by Dave Braun and Troy Amdahl

The Art of Stillness by Pico Iyer

INSPIRATION AND GIVING BACK

Writing this book was step one of my plan. Getting over the fear that "I'm not a writer" was my first step toward doing what was on my bucket list for years. I have been telling myself that I wasn't good at writing, so I can't write a book. That's ridiculous. Writing is subjective, just like music, poetry, and art. It's all in the eye of the beholder. Who is a writer anyway? A writer is someone who writes. Well, then I can say I am a writer. I wrote this book. I hope to sell millions of copies but not for financial gain. Instead, in step two of my plan, I will take a portion of the proceeds and donate to a charity. However, not just any charity because I want to create one myself. I will admit that watching Ellen over the years has inspired me to be more generous and kinder. I admire how she ends all of her shows, reminding us to be kind to one another. It's such a powerful message that I don't think everyone takes to heart. I feel that this world needs more kindness. If people felt good about themselves, I think we'd be a little kinder to each other. If we feel a little

A SIMPLE SOUL

more love, maybe we'd love each other more. I want to create a charity where I can make people smile and warm their hearts, even if it's just for a moment. It'll be a charity based on the idea of kindness.

If I ever win the lottery, which I never play, I wouldn't change a thing in my life. I am so content and at peace that nothing I could buy would make me happier. But there are two things I would do:

1. Get a massage once a week for the rest of my life and
2. Do random acts of kindness every day. So, suppose I do sell millions of copies of this book. In that case, I will have the platform and the financial opportunity to do random acts of kindness. I want to take a portion of whatever I make and create a charity called RUA-OK Corporation.

Are you a-okay? It stands for Random Unexpected Acts Of Kindness. I will use the money to go around town doing random acts of kindness...paying for someone's groceries, buying someone's coffee, picking up the tab at a restaurant for a stranger, etc. You get the idea. I thought if I ever won the lottery, I would do this. Still, the proceeds of my book may offer a perfect opportunity for me to create this platform to do good by making others smile. We need to smile more and feel love. I know it's temporary happiness, and I'm not dramatically changing lives, but just the act of kindness can warm our hearts. I love the idea of paying it forward. One simple act of kindness may inspire that person to do an act of kindness for a stranger and so on. Love is contagious. So are kindness and generosity.

So, the more books I sell, the more kindness will go around. I have no doubt that at least one of the messages in this book touched you or hit a cord, or possibly even inspired you to be a better version of yourself. As an instructor, my job is to reach people with my message, even if it's just one person. I don't think that anything I talked about is necessarily a revelation but just a reminder. We need reminders to keep life in perspective. If you didn't get anything out of any of the messages or lessons I've learned through my years, please know this. You are AMAZING just the way you are. Our souls are perfect the way they are. Our egos get in the way. Please be mindful of what you invite into your world and of your thoughts, actions, behaviors.

 A SIMPLE SOUL

"Your beliefs become your thoughts,

Your thoughts become your words,

Your words become your actions,

Your actions become your habits,

Your habits become your values,

Your values become your destiny."

—Mahatma Gandhi

ACKNOWLEDGMENTS

Writing this book has been a journey in itself. I am eternally grateful for the love and support I have in my life. My mother has always loved and supported me in all of my adventures and experiences. Both good and bad, she has been there for me through it all. Even though my dad is no longer with me here on earth, he gave me many blessings that I carry in my heart. Thank you, Mom and Dad, for your support.

My daughter, Olivia, and my son, Jackson, inspire me and motivate me to stay positive through the peaks and valleys of life. Being the mother to these two has been one of the best gifts that life has given me. I am honored to be their mother, and their love and support through this process has been a blessing. Thank you, Sunshines.

I thank my editor, Linda Tucker, who patiently guided me through this adventure. Without her help, I'm not sure this book would have happened. Thank you for your hard work, Linda! Your effort is truly appreciated.

A SIMPLE SOUL

Finally, every person in my life has influenced me in some way. I thank my family and friends, both close and distant, for making me the person I am. You have supported me through my endless journeys. Your kindness, love, and support don't go unrecognized. With a sincere heart, I thank you.

Made in the USA
Las Vegas, NV
15 May 2021